CW00403752

TEACHING CHILDREN & YOUNG PEOPLE *with* SPECIAL EDUCATIONAL NEEDS & DISABILITIES

SAGE was founded in 1965 by Sara Miller McCune to support the dissemination of usable knowledge by publishing innovative and high-quality research and teaching content. Today, we publish more than 750 journals, including those of more than 300 learned societies, more than 800 new books per year, and a growing range of library products including archives, data, case studies, reports, conference highlights, and video. SAGE remains majority-owned by our founder, and on her passing will become owned by a charitable trust that secures our continued independence.

Los Angeles | London | Washington DC | New Delhi | Singapore

TEACHING CHILDREN & YOUNG PEOPLE with SPECIAL EDUCATIONAL NEEDS & DISABILITIES

edited by

→ SARAH MARTIN-DENHAM

SAGE

Los Angeles | London | New Delhi
Singapore | Washington DC

Los Angeles | London | New Delhi
Singapore | Washington DC

SAGE Publications Ltd
1 Oliver's Yard
55 City Road
London EC1Y 1SP

SAGE Publications Inc.
2455 Teller Road
Thousand Oaks, California 91320

SAGE Publications India Pvt Ltd
B 1/I 1 Mohan Cooperative Industrial Area
Mathura Road
New Delhi 110 044

SAGE Publications Asia-Pacific Pte Ltd
3 Church Street
#10-04 Samsung Hub
Singapore 049483

Editor: Jude Bowen/Amy Jarrold
Editorial assistant: George Knowles
Production editor: Nicola Marshall
Copyeditor: Solveig Gardner Servian
Proofreader: Mary Dalton
Indexer: Silvia Benvenuto
Marketing executive: Dilhara Attygalle
Cover design: Wendy Scott
Typeset by: C&M Digitals (P) Ltd, Chennai, India
Printed and bound by CPI Group (UK) Ltd,
Croydon, CR0 4YY

Library of Congress Control Number: 2014944801

British Library Cataloguing in Publication data

A catalogue record for this book is available from the British Library

MIX
Paper from
responsible sources
FSC
www.fsc.org FSC® C013604

ISBN 978-1-44629-432-1
ISBN 978-1-44629-433-8 (pbk)

At SAGE we take sustainability seriously. Most of our products are printed in the UK using FSC papers and boards.
When we print overseas we ensure sustainable papers are used as measured by the Egmont grading system.
We undertake an annual audit to monitor our sustainability.

CONTENTS

ABOUT THE EDITOR

Sarah Martin-Denham is a Senior Lecturer at the University of Sunderland. She has extensive knowledge of teaching in the North East of England in a variety of settings ranging from Early Years to post 16, where she has developed a particular interest and expertise in special educational needs. Sarah currently teaches on the primary initial teacher training programmes and supports trainees whilst they are on placement in a range of mainstream and specialist contexts. She also leads and teaches on the MA Special Needs and Inclusive Education programme and the National Award for Special Educational Needs Co-ordination.

ABOUT THE CONTRIBUTORS

Bill Ashton

Bill has worked in mainstream and special schools for 37 years. For the most part he has specialised in working with young people with emotional, social and behavioural difficulties (ESBD). Bill was a special educational needs co-ordinator for 28 years; during that time he established units in mainstream schools for ESBD, the visually impaired and hearing impaired and deaf children. He regularly delivers training on behaviour management in mainstream and special schools. He has made a study of attachment and relational trauma and the effects on teaching and learning. He now operates two children's homes in the borough of Redcar.

Judith Donovan

Judith is Deputy Head Teacher at Gibside special school in Gateshead. During her extensive career teaching Physical Education and Mathematics in secondary mainstream, then teaching in Further Education, and in her current role, she has gained extensive experience in teaching pupils with special educational needs and disabilities. Judith is highly regarded in teacher training and continues to have a positive impact on the quality of new teachers.

Rebecca Dunn

Following her university degree, Rebecca has completed her first year of teaching in Key Stage 1 in mainstream provision. At university she developed a particular passion for the inclusion of children with special needs in mainstream contexts. She strongly believes that all children have the right to a motivating and challenging curriculum and strives to achieve this as a teacher.

Dawn Henderson

After spending her early teaching years as a secondary mainstream teacher of science, Dawn moved into a specialist setting and has been teaching young people with special educational needs and disabilities for 14 years. Through her role as Professional Lead for North East Special Schools Teaching Partnership, Dawn has a specific focus of supporting the training and development of professionals working in specialist settings. She has a particular interest in developing the skills, knowledge and experience of training teachers in preparation for working with children and young people with a range of learning difficulties and challenges.

Karen Horridge

Karen is Consultant Paediatrician (Disability), City Hospitals Sunderland NHS Foundation Trust. Karen has 20 years' experience in providing healthcare for disabled children and young people. She led on development of the subspecialty of paediatric neurodisability at the Royal College of Paediatrics and Child Health, is Chair of the British Academy of Childhood Disability (UK) and is leading on development of e-learning materials aiming to challenge and positively change attitudes towards disabled children and young people in our society.

Helen Irving

Helen has over 40 years' experience in teaching in both mainstream and specialist schools across all the age phases, and supporting teachers and pupils as a member of a Special Educational Needs support service. She later became an advisory teacher, training manager, and trainer for SEN within her local authority, where she was the named specialist teacher for dyslexia, following her award of Postgraduate Certificate in Specific Learning Difficulties and becoming an Associate Member of The British Dyslexia Association in 1999. Since then she has also worked as mentor, assessor and tutor on programmes related to dyslexia to Masters Level.

Pauline James

Pauline is Deputy Head of Villa Real School in County Durham, which is a specialist school for pupils aged 2–19 with severe and complex learning difficulties, challenging behaviour and autism. She has taught school leavers for many years and is particularly concerned that pupils' achievements are celebrated, and that pupils are well prepared to take their place as valuable, and valued, citizens in the outside world. As a keen musician, she is also leader of the Villa Real Handchimes Group.

Jayne Littlewood

Since graduating nearly 20 years ago Jayne has worked as a teacher in primary special education, predominantly with children who have a diagnosis of autism. Jayne is particularly interested in working with children who display very challenging behaviour and working with non-verbal children focusing on approaches to develop their communication skills and their need/desire to communicate.

Helen Lowes

Helen Lowes teaches in a large mainstream primary school. Her interest within special educational needs became apparent when she voluntarily worked in a specialist provision alongside children with attachment difficulties and autism. She believes that every child has the right to learn and access a high-quality education regardless of their ability or need.

Denise Murray

Denise is Assistant Head Teacher and Special Educational Needs Co-ordinator at Barbara Priestman Academy in Sunderland. She has taught in a range of specialist contexts teaching pupils age 2–19 years. Denise is passionate and enthusiastic about extra-curricular activities such as summer and residential schools to promote positive relationships with hard to reach young people. She is highly regarded in the training she provides for autism and managing pupil behaviour for local schools and colleges.

David Nevins

Since graduating with his BA (Hons) Primary, David is teaching in a mainstream primary school in the North East of England and has a passion for teaching and supporting children with special educational needs. Through his university studies he has developed a particular interest in accommodating for the needs of children diagnosed with dyslexia and autism.

Jan Patterson

Jan undertook specialist initial teacher training for teaching children with special educational needs. She has taught across the North East in special schools for pupils with severe learning difficulties, profound and multiple learning difficulties, complex medical needs and physical disabilities. She has taught across all ages, starting in post 16 and has specialised in early years for the past 28 years.

Chris Roberts

Chris is a teacher in the Complex and Additional Needs Department at Horizons Specialist Academy Trust in Stockton-on-Tees. Joining the school in 2006 after a varied career, he gained a passion for teaching pupils with severe learning difficulties. Working closely with the speech and language therapist he created a group within the department that focused on developing and promoting communication. He has presented at a Communication Matters Conference and has developed close links with the University of Sunderland as a specialist in special educational needs.

Claire Sewell

Claire is currently working within the Initial Teacher Education sector. Since graduating she has worked in both primary mainstream and specialist educational provision in both the Midlands and the North East. Her passion for teaching children and young people is derived from her desire to support them in meeting their true potential. She has a particular interest in working with children on the autistic spectrum and with those that present with very challenging behaviours. Her research into how professionals can support families with children with SEN derived from her experience of working in specialist provision and seeing how a little support could go a long way.

Steve Siddell

Steve is a Head Teacher; he has been teaching and learning from young people for 29 years. Following five years in industry he decided that he was far more interested in working with children than with noxious chemicals. Steve believes in some simple and deep ideas: that children are people, that secure attachments are essential in childhood and 'that putting all the difficult children in one place (Pupil Referral Units) and imagining this will solve anything' lacks either common sense or honesty.

Caroline Walker-Gleaves

Caroline is Senior Lecturer in Special Education and Inclusion at Durham University. Caroline has a doctorate in Education, specialising in caring pedagogical approaches to facilitate inclusion. On the basis of her work in this field, Caroline was in 2001, awarded a HEFCE National Teaching Fellowship and in 2005, she was nominated for the Ernest L. Boyer International Award for Outstanding Pedagogic Scholarship. In 2013 and 2014, she won Vice Chancellor's Awards for Outstanding Teaching and Doctoral Supervison in the area of Special Education.

James Waller

James is Assistant Head Teacher at Sunningdale special school in Sunderland. He manages two specialist support services for Sunderland Local Authority: The Language & Learning Partnership and the Sunderland Portage Service. He has worked in both Primary phase special education and all-age (2–19) phase special education, from the Early Years to Key Stage 5. James has also worked with the Newcastle-based outreach support charity, The Coquet Trust and coached the Newcastle Council Disability football team.

The contributors Chris and Jan and the editor would like to extend their thanks to **Sue Rowney** and **Elisa Liu**, speech and language therapists, for their advice and guidance on Chapter 9, Speech, Language and Communication Needs.

ACKNOWLEDGEMENTS

I would like to give my sincere thanks to the inspirational and devoted contributors in this book without whom it could not have been possible. You have all made and continue to make a difference to the lives and aspirations of children and young people.

I would also like to thank my family for their relentless support and encouragement. Particularly to my parents Judy and Paul for believing in me when they were continuously told I would never achieve anything by my primary school teachers. To Mum and Dad I owe you so much. Thank you to my husband Ben and sister Lucy who have been supportive every step of the way and to my two little treasures Emily and William for giving your Mum time to do this book.

I would also like to thank Jude Bowen and Amy Jarrold at SAGE for their ongoing support and encouragement.

Thanks to you all.

Sarah Martin-Denham

SAGE and the editor would also like to thank Mayer-Johnson for their permission to include Figures 9.2–9.6.
Mayer-Johnson
2100 Wharton Street
Suite 400
Pittsburgh, PA 15203

Phone: 1 (800) 588-4548
Fax: 1 (866) 585-6260

Email: *mayer-johnson.usa@mayer-johnson.com*
Web site: *www.mayer-johnson.com*

PREFACE

The aim of this practical guide is to enable trainee teachers, practising teachers and support staff to develop their knowledge and understanding of how to effectively promote teaching and learning in a specialist or mainstream provision for children and young people from 0–25 years. The book will support teaching in a range of contexts including specialist and mainstream primary and secondary schools, pupil referral units, resource/specialist based provisions attached to mainstream schools and residential schools and those teaching in the further education sector.

This book has been written by a range of experts in the field of special educational needs who are currently working or who have worked with vulnerable children across the age phases early years to post 16. Their extensive knowledge and understanding of teaching and learning has resulted in a comprehensive guide to supporting those who are embarking on or who are currently teaching in a specialist context or indeed for those working in a mainstream provision. The book also includes guidance from those employed within the health services who offer specific advice and guidance in teaching those with disabilities. The book will be useful to those who are on teaching practice as part of their teacher training and for teachers and support staff who are teaching in a specialist or mainstream context for the first time.

It is hoped that by the end of this book you will be able to confidently teach pupils with a range of areas of exceptionality. This book will share teaching strategies to allow you to engage with often hard to reach learners. Before you can begin teaching pupils with special educational needs and/or disabilities you need to understand their holistic needs. Therefore, this book focuses on supporting the whole child or young person in collaboration with their families and other professionals who are involved with their education and care.

For the purpose of this book and for ease of reading, the term 'pupil' will be used throughout to refer to all children and young people from

5–25 years. There will of course be exceptions to this where the reference is to children in the EYFS (0–5 years) and in relation to the views of parents and looked after children.

Chapter features

Within each of the chapters there will be a consistent structure. At the beginning of each chapter you will see 'Key ideas explored in this chapter'. This sets out a series of statements which refer to the chapter content and the expected learning you will acquire. Embedded in each chapter you will also find case studies from the practitioners and reflective activities for you to consider in light of the content. The case studies and reflective accounts are all based on real situations/experiences; however, the names used are fictitious. Each chapter will close with suggested additional resources that the contributors and I recommend you read/access. These will be essential to further develop your knowledge and understanding of the particular needs and requirements of the pupils you teach.

Online extras

Additional materials have kindly been supplied by Gibside School, Gateshead and Judith Donovan, and can be found at **www.sagepub.co.uk/martindenham**. These include exemplar learning and behaviour plans, level descriptors and schemes of work for teaching pupils with special educational needs and disabilities.

ACRONYMS AND ABBREVIATIONS

AAC	Augmentative and Alternative Communication
ADD	Attention Deficit Disorder
ADHD	Attention Deficit Hyperactivity Disorder
AfL	Assessment for Learning
APP	Assessing Pupil Progress
ASC	Autistic Spectrum Condition
ASDAN	Award Scheme Development and Accreditation Network
BSL	British Sign Language
CAMHS	Child and Adolescent Mental Health Services
CASPA	Comparison and Analysis of Special Pupil Attainment
CF	Cystic Fibrosis
CSW	Curriculum Support Worker
DBS	Disclosure and Barring Service
DfE	Department for Education
DO	Designated Officer
EAL	English as an Additional Language
EHC	Education, Health and Care plan
EQUALS	Entitlement and Quality Education for Pupils with Learning Difficulties
ESBD	Emotional, Social and Behavioural Difficulties
EYFS	Early Years Foundation Stage
FE	Further Education
FSM	Free School Meals
GCSE	General Certificate in Secondary Education
GDD	Global Development Delay
GP	General Practitioner
HI	Hearing Impairment
HLTA	Higher Level Teaching Assistant
ICT	Information and Communications Technology

LA	Local Authority
LLE	Local Leader of Education
LTP	Long-term Planning
MLD	Moderate Learning Difficulties
MSI	Multi-sensory Impairment
MTP	Medium-term Planning
NALDIC	National Association for Language Development in the Curriculum
NC	National Curriculum
NHS	National Health Service
NLE	National Leader of Education
NNEB	National Nursery Examination Board
NQT	Newly Qualified Teacher
NVQ	National Vocational Qualifications
OCD	Obsessive Compulsive Disorder
Ofsted	Office for Standards in Education
PCS™	Picture Communication Symbols
PDA	Pathological Demand Avoidance
PECS®	Picture Exchange Communication System
PIVATS	Performance Indicators for Value Added Target Setting
PMLD	Profound and Multiple Learning Difficulties
PRU	Pupil Referral Unit
PSHE	Personal, Social and Health Education
SA	Support Assistant
SATs	Standard Assessment Tests
SCERTS	Social Communication, Emotional Regulation and Transactional Support
SEN	Special Educational Needs
SENCO	Special Educational Needs Co-ordinator
SEND	Special Educational Needs and/or Disability
SIO	School Improvement Officers
SLCN	Speech, Language and Communication Needs
SLD	Severe Learning Difficulty
SLT	Speech and Language Therapist
SNA	Special Needs Assistant
SoW	Scheme of Work
SpLD	Specific Learning Difficulty
SSA	Specialist Support Assistant
STP	Short-term Planning
TA	Teaching Assistant
Tacpac®	Tactile Approach to Communication Pack
VI	Visual Impairment
VOCA	Voice Output Communication Aids
WLS™	Widgit Symbols

CHAPTER 1

INTRODUCTION

Sarah Martin-Denham

Key ideas explored in this chapter

- What are Special Educational Needs (SEN)?
- What is a disability?
- What were the key reforms in September 2014?
- What is SEN support?
- What are Education, Health and Care plans (EHCs)?
- The four broad areas of need
- What are personal budgets and direct payments?
- The local offer
- Final thoughts

This chapter will outline the key government reforms to special educational needs and/or disabilities (SEND) that were enshrined in part 3 of the Children and Families Act 2014 and the guidance within the *Special Educational Needs and Disability Code of Practice* (DfE, 2014a). The SEND legislation has introduced many changes, including integrated assessment and planning from 0–25 years across education, health and social care with a focus on long-term outcomes. Education, Health and Care plans (EHCs) have replaced Statements of SEN for those with more complex needs who require a personalised approach. SEN support refers to those children or young people who have SEN but don't require a statutory assessment and don't have an EHC plan in place. The needs of all pupils with SEND have to be met through inclusive high-quality teaching, differentiated to their particular needs. Schools are required to use their best endeavours to make sure those with SEND get the necessary support they need. There is an emphasis on drawing on the views of parents and carers and the full involvement of them and the child/young person in terms of providing for their needs.

What are Special Educational Needs (SEN)?

The *Special Educational Needs and Disability Code of Practice* (DfE, 2014a) defines SEN as: 'a child or young person has SEN if they have a learning difficulty or disability which calls for special educational needs provision to be made for him or her.' This refers to any education or training provision which is additional to or different from that generally provided for others of the same age. The local authority (LA) has to ensure that those with SEN or a disability receive education and training that allows them to 'achieve the best possible education and other outcomes' (HM Government, 2014a). The majority of children with SEN and disabilities will have their needs met in mainstream provision.

What is a disability?

A disability is 'a physical or mental impairment which has a long term and substantial adverse effect on their ability to carry out normal day to day activities' (DfE, 2014a, p. 5). 'Long term' is defined as a year or more and 'substantial' is defined as 'more than minor than trivial'. Disability includes sensory impairments such as those impacting on sight and hearing and long-term health conditions such as asthma, diabetes, epilepsy and cancer. If a child with a disability also requires special educational provision, they are also covered by the definition for SEN.

What were the key reforms in September 2014?

The Children and Families Act (HM Government, 2014a) legislated key reforms which have changed the way we plan for the needs of pupils SEND as outlined in the *Special Educational Needs and Disability Code of*

Practice (DfE, 2014a). The focus of the changes was to develop the strategic effectiveness of all education contexts to raise outcomes for all children and young people from 0–25 years. Providers will have a duty to ensure that they identify and address the SEN and/or diasa-bilities of those that they are supporting/teaching and use their best endeavours to make sure their needs are met. There are two levels of SEN: those who will have an EHC plan, and those with a lesser level of need who receive SEN support.

What is SEN support?

If it becomes apparent that a child in the early years is not meeting expected levels of progress, practitioners and the special educational needs co-ordinator (SENCO) in the setting need to gather information on the child's learning and development in relation to the prime areas of communication and language, physical development and personal, social and emotional development. This information alongside spe-cialist advice from other professionals, if appropriate, should be used to ascertain whether the child has SEN. This should be carried out with the full collaboration of the parents/carers. If a child is not achieving expected outcomes it is important to note that they may not have SEN as defined on page 2. There can be many causal factors such as the home environment, poverty and family circumstances. It could also be the case that the child's first language is not English – difficulties arising in relation to learning English as an additional language (EAL) does not equate to the child or young person having special educational needs.

Those children who have SEN support following stringent identifica-tion and assessment but who continue to not make expected progress, may then move towards having a statutory assessment for an EHC plan. The role of the SENCO in educational contexts is to ensure that all practitioners understand the approach to identifying and meet-ing the needs of pupils with SEN. They will be able to provide advice and support to you as a teacher in the school and share information (where appropriate) regarding which agencies support the pupils you are working with and why.

SEN support in schools has a focus on removing barriers to learning and addressing potential areas of difficulty in the lessons that you teach. This can only be achieved when you have a full understanding of the pupils' needs (in depth) and how they learn and incorporate this into your provision for that pupil. The cycle of support is known as the gradu-ated approach of 'assess, plan, do and review'. By reading Chapters 4, 5 and 6 you will understand how this is used in your day-to-day teaching. If there are concerns about a child's progress, then information should be gathered by the teacher and SENCO. The information should include an early discussion with the pupil and their parents to identify their strengths, difficulties, concerns, agreed outcomes and next steps.

What are Education, Health and Care plans (EHCs)?

Some children and young people will need an EHC plan to secure the best possible outcomes for them in terms of their education, health and social care as they move into adulthood. The purpose of the EHC plan is to establish the views, interests and aspirations of the parents and the child or young person. It outlines their particular needs and includes the provision they require to allow them to achieve the agreed outcomes. Parents can request an assessment from the LA for an EHC plan assessment once a child is born. Young people from 16 years of age but under the age of 25 can also request an assessment independently and can do this with the support of an advocate. It is important to note that a range of professionals across health, education and social care can refer children for an EHC plan assessment, which should be done with the agreement and in collaboration with the parents/carers, and that it must be completed within 20 weeks.

The content of the EHC plan includes:

- the views, interests and aspirations of the child, their parents or young person;
- an outline of their SEN and/or disabilities;
- their particular health needs which are related to their SEN;
- their social care needs which are related to their SEN or disability;
- the outcomes sought for them, including outcomes for adult life – it must identify arrangements for setting shorter-term targets by the early years, school or college provider;
- the special educational provision required;
- any health provision required by the learning difficulties or disabilities – this may include an 'individual health care plan';
- any social care provision;
- the name and type of the school to be attended;
- if appropriate, details of how the personal budget will support particular outcomes, the provision it will be used for and any arrangements for direct payments;
- any advice and information gathered during the EHC plan needs assessment must be attached.

The four broad areas of need

The SEN and disability code of practice 0–25 years outlines four broad areas. There will be children and young people who do not fit neatly into one category, others whose needs are across the areas (e.g. those with autism), and of course needs may change over time.

1. **Communication and interaction:** This includes those with speech, language and communication needs (SLCN) who find communicating with others difficult. This also applies to children and young people with autism and Asperger's syndrome who encounter challenges with social interaction, language, communication and imagination.
2. **Cognition and learning:** This includes moderate and severe learning difficulties (SLD) through to profound and multiple learning difficulties (PMLD) resulting in support being needed to access all areas of the curriculum. In addition this includes specific learning difficulties (SpLD) such as dyslexia, dyscalculia and dyspraxia that make learning challenging even with appropriate differentiation.
3. **Social, emotional and mental health difficulties:** These difficulties can present in a range of ways and will be unique to the individual child or young person. They may become withdrawn, challenging, disruptive, isolated or demonstrate other concerning behaviours. When these behaviours are presenting it may be symptomatic of underlying mental health difficulties such as depression, eating disorders, self-harming, substance abuse, anxiety or depression. This broad area also includes attention deficit disorder (ADD), attention deficit hyperactivity disorder (ADHD) or attachment difficulties. It is important to highlight that behaviour is not a category. The role of the practitioner is to find out the reasons behind the behaviours that the pupil is presenting. They could be the result of a range of causal factors such as social difficulties, their home life, SpLD or as a result of their mental health.
4. **Sensory and/or physical needs:** This includes children and young people who require special educational provision because of their disability. This includes vision and/or hearing impairment, multi-sensory impairment, and some children with a physical disability who may require additional support to access all the opportunities available to their peers.

What are personal budgets and direct payments?

Once there is a draft EHC plan and it has been issued to parents or a young person, they can request that a personal budget is prepared for them. The personal budget is a notional amount of money that can be used to secure provision outlined in the EHC plan. Parents and young people can ask that part of the personal budget is in the form of a direct payment made to them so they can directly commission and manage services themselves.

The local offer

The local offer is devised by the LA and sets out the universal support expected to be available across health, education and social care for all children with SEND. The intended purpose of this is to provide up-to-date, clear and comprehensible information about the range of provision and how to access it. The local offer will also include guidance to parents and carers about how to request an assessment for an EHC plan with the identification and assessment process. As there is no set format, the local offer for each LA will vary in terms of how it is presented on their website so it is worth looking at the area you will be teaching in. The challenge will be keeping the local offer up to date and gaining feedback from families who are accessing it.

Final thoughts

I hope that the reforms are positive and that the four-part cycle of 'assess, plan, do and review' is implemented in all educational contexts in a timely manner when it is evident that a child or young person is experiencing challenges in their learning and development. My concern is that there will be educational contexts and LAs who are not equipped financially, or do not have time to thoroughly complete the first step.

My personal concerns are for those who do not meet the threshold for an EHC plan who will be in the school-based category of SEN support. This seems to be the area of the code of practice which lacks rigour and detail. From ongoing personal experience of knowing a child with difficulties which became apparent at the age of seven to discover she is still not entitled to be screened for specific learning difficulties at the age of 11 would suggest not. It seems that children have to fail before a full assessment of their needs begins. The parent of the child was told by a LA that for her to be screened for a SpLD she needed be two levels 'behind' in terms of national expectations. She was a level 3 in mathematics in Y6 and even though the school agreed with the parents that she had underlying difficulties with calculation and working memory, the LA would not involve their services unless she was a level 2. It was instead suggested that the parent wait until she entered Key Stage 3 because her profile would look worse as she was no longer in primary provision.

Imagine a world where children and young people have the assessment and identification as soon as it is needed. Then you would know the specific challenges they encounter, the gaps in their learning and their learning preferences. Follow this with accommodation of their strengths, needs, abilities and interests through inclusive quality first teaching in the classroom and who knows, they may thrive and surpass expectations.

Fingers crossed that once the reforms are embedded they will make a positive difference to all children and young people with SEND.

Additional resources

As well as the resources you'll find at **www.sagepub.co.uk/martindenham** you should also take a look at the following:

The SEND Gateway NASEN, www.sendgateway.org.uk/: This website provides education professionals free, easy access to high-quality information, resources and training for meeting the needs of children with SEND.

Department for Education (DfE) (2014a) *Special Educational Needs and Disability Code of Practice: 0–25 Years*. London: DfE. This statutory guidance includes duties, policies and procedures relating to Part 3 of the Children and Families Act 2014. This is essential reading for those working with children and young people with SEND. The reforms to SEND provision are too great to include fully in this introduction. This guidance is essential reading.

HM Government (2014a) *The Children and Families Act 2014*. London: The Stationery Office. This is the Act of parliament through which the SEN reforms were enshrined in law.

CHAPTER 2

WHO'S WHO IN SPECIALIST PROVISION?

Jan Patterson and James Waller

Key ideas explored in this chapter

- School staffing structure
- Roles and responsibilities in specialist contexts
- Professionals you will work with
- Multi-agency teams
- The role of health professionals
- The role of social care teams
- Private and charitable support

School staffing structure

As has been mentioned in the introduction, there are a variety of different types of specialist provision depending on the requirements of each Local Authority (LA). Similarly school leadership, staffing structures, support services and multi-agency partnerships vary from area to area and even school to school. Some of these are explicit (e.g. members of the school leadership team or who the support staff are) whilst other aspects of these structures or relationships may be unspoken and less formal. As with any teaching role, it will be of paramount importance to be familiar with the relationships and support available in the specialist school setting. Whilst structures and relationships may vary, many roles and professionals that are encountered will be the same. Understanding the roles and responsibilities of these professionals will make navigating the less explicit working relationships far simpler.

Roles and responsibilities in specialist contexts

The senior leadership team in a specialist school will, on paper, appear a little different from that of any mainstream primary or secondary school. There will be a head teacher, principals or executive head teacher who is supported by some combination of head teachers, deputy head teachers and assistant head teachers or even vice principals. This will vary based on the needs of the school and what their roles are. Ultimately these people will lead and manage the school. A vast number of responsibilities will be shared amongst these professionals.

Additional responsibilities may arise through Teaching School or National Support School commitments, Local Leader of Education (LLE) and National Leader of Education (NLE) responsibilities resulting in work with other schools, school leaders or LAs. Senior leaders may also take on many functions usually associated with a special educational needs co-ordinator (SENCO) in a mainstream school such as preparing for a statutory assessment by the LA, chairing annual review meetings or a pupil's EHC plan. It is important to note that a specialist school may not have a designated SENCO in the same way that a mainstream school would.

Teachers in specialist provisions are generally employed under the same terms and conditions as their mainstream colleagues and are required to meet the *Teachers' Standards* (DfE, 2011a). The roles and responsibilities will vary significantly across differing provisions. The key difference is that as a teacher in specialist provision you will rarely, if ever, work alone in a classroom with pupils. It is a team role working very closely with pupils, parents and other professionals. The same career structure applies; however, until recently there were few newly qualified teachers (NQTs) employed in specialist provision.

The majority of pupils in specialist provision will have an EHC plan, which needs to be considered in their individual learning plans to improve their outcomes. You will be responsible for planning and delivering the Early Years Foundation Stage (EYFS), National Curriculum or post

16 curriculum, adapted, modified and possibly extended to meet the identified individual needs of the pupils that you teach.

Professionals you will work with

Support staff have many titles and roles within specialist provisions; they may also have a wide range of qualifications, including National Nursery Examination Board (NNEB) and/or National Vocational Qualifications (NVQ). As in mainstream provision, their job titles may be Teaching Assistant (TA), Higher Level Teaching Assistant (HLTA) and Lunchtime Supervisor. In specialist provision they may have titles such as Specialist Support Assistant or Special Needs Assistant (SSA/SNA), Curriculum Support Worker (CSW). Their roles may vary greatly in each specialist context; however, their main duties are to provide additional support to meet pupils' individual needs. In some specialist contexts support staff are encouraged to undergo further training, either 'in house' or from training providers, to take on additional roles and responsibilities, particularly additional therapies such as rebound therapy, hydrotherapy, sound therapy and light room therapy. Other support may come from professionals external to the educational context.

If you work with younger pupils you may encounter the Portage Service. This is a home-based service for pre-school pupils with significant additional needs. Portage home visitors assess the needs of the child and work in partnership with their parents to build on their abilities and develop new skills. The portage home visitor then outlines carefully structured activities to enable parents to support and encourage effective learning for their child. For a three-year-old pupil starting school or nursery with a moderate (MLD), severe (SLD) or profound and multiple (PMLD) learning difficulties, the portage home visitor can be a valuable source of advice and information about the pupil's needs and abilities.

As a pupil with SEN becomes older they will receive input from the Connexions service. Connexions provides additional support for young people with learning difficulties up to the age of 25. A Connexions advisor would usually become involved with the pupil from the end of Key Stage 3 onwards. They will attend annual review meetings, offer advice to parents and schools about future school placements/college and potential work opportunities, and will accompany the pupil and their parents on visits to colleges, schools, training providers and employers. They will support pupils, families and school staff with applications and interviews and endeavour to facilitate smooth transitions between settings.

Pupils with certain sensory impairments will receive input from the hearing impaired or visually impaired service. Teachers who work for the service support visually impaired (VI) and hearing impaired (HI) pupils, providing advice and intervention for those with sensory impairments in both specialist and mainstream contexts.

Many LAs have specialist language support services which are available to support difficulties encountered by specific pupils (e.g. The Language and Learning Partnership and The Complex Language and Learning Service).

Some pupils with autism will attend specialist provision, but in many cases autism is only one of several diagnoses that a pupil with additional needs might have. In these cases the pupil may attend a school that meets their predominant need. Services such as the autism outreach team in Sunderland consist of class teachers, support workers and TAs trained in all aspects of autism, and they will use and advise on a number of specialist teaching techniques such as Tacpac® and PECS®, Social Stories™ and other similar interventions.

Multi-agency teams

As a teacher in the education sector there will be a number of professionals external to the school that you will work alongside. The LA will usually have some form of school improvement team. Although they may have a number of job titles, this team will include a number of School Improvement Officers (SIO) who will use their skills, experience and expertise to offer support in a number of curriculum areas including SEND. These individuals will usually work closely with senior and middle leadership or subject co-ordinators to offer guidance and to develop specific areas within school.

The role of health professionals

There are a range of health professionals who will be supporting the pupils you are teaching. Therapists are generally employed by NHS Trusts and may work within specialist provision, providing ongoing advice and support to both staff, pupils and parents. There may be therapist provision specified within the EHC plans which needs to be incorporated into the pupil's daily programmes of work.

Specialist speech and language therapists (SLTs) work closely with teachers and support staff in specialist provision to plan and advise on all aspects of language development and communication, including communication aids. They may work with individual pupils or groups. However, more recently their role is increasingly advisory, and staff working directly with pupils implement programmes and approaches following their advice. Some SLTs have additional training and guidance on eating and drinking issues.

Physiotherapists (often referred to as 'physios') work with pupils with physical disabilities. There may also be physiotherapy technicians and assistants who work under the guidance of a qualified physiotherapist, implementing programmes with individual pupils in specialist contexts.

In specialist contexts where pupils have additional medical needs there may be a school nurse who is based in the provision. They are employed by the NHS Trusts and will generally be specially trained staff nurses.

The role of the school nurse may include:

- administering medication;
- supporting school staff with medical matters concerning the pupils;
- carrying out health assessments and developmental screening;
- linking with other health professionals and attending multi-professional meetings.

There are also a range of specialist medical health professionals that you may encounter when working in specialist provision, particularly with pupils with complex medical needs. These include children's community nurse specialists who work closely with specialist consultant paediatricians to link with families and schools for those pupils who have ongoing medical needs. There are also children's continence nurse specialists (who can advise on provision of nappies and other continence issues), children's epilepsy nurse specialists, children's gastroenterology nurse specialists, therapists, dieticians and specialist health visitors.

The Child and Adolescent Mental Health Services (CAMHS) are part of the National Health Service (NHS) and specialise in providing assistance and treatment for pupils and young people with emotional, behavioural and mental health difficulties. CAMHS will provide support that is useful in both school and the pupil's home. Some LAs offer specialist behaviour support services that work similarly to CAMHS but specifically in schools. These specialists can be particularly useful in supporting with the implementation of simple behaviour support strategies for individual or groups of pupils.

As well as ongoing support and input from services such as physiotherapy and speech and language therapy, there are a number of services that may be referred to or become involved with a pupil because of a specific set of circumstances.

The role of social care teams

The makeup of social care teams will be different in different areas; there will be general similarities in the work they do. They will provide a service for families with a child/pupil aged 0–25 years who as a result of a disability needs a higher level of care than a pupil without disabilities of similar age and circumstances. Cases are likely to be taken on a referral basis and will commence through an initial assessment by a key worker, sometimes called a 'key person'.

Social care professionals may recommend the following services:

- referral to other professionals such as psychologists or paediatric nurses;
- support in the home or community;
- an occupational therapist assessment for equipment and/or adaptations;
- short breaks, either family based or residential.

Educational psychologists will generally be involved in assessing the learning and emotional needs of pupils. These are carried out by observing the pupil and then consulting with multi-agency teams to advise on the best approaches and provisions to support their learning and development. Educational psychologists will be involved in developing and supporting therapeutic and behaviour management programmes and will also contribute towards the EHC plan. A school may be assigned a 'patch' educational psychologist (who work across a number of provisions in a geographical area), but it is also possible to pay for additional support from private educational psychologists.

Occupational therapists are employed by NHS Trusts and work closely with schools, families and children to support them in overcoming the effects of disability so that they can participate in daily life. They will advise schools on equipment individual pupils need such as walking frames, wheelchairs and writing slopes, and how to adapt the school environment to improve accessibility and independence.

Private and charitable support

The private and charitable support network for pupils with specific, severe, moderate, profound and multiple, emotional, behavioural and complex difficulties is widespread and is continuing to grow. It is possible that whilst teaching in a specialist provision you will encounter various professional adults who make up the support team that surrounds a pupil who you work with. These may include outreach support workers, charities, specialist private teachers, private consultants, respite workers, learning mentors and coaches of various descriptions. It is important to foster strong working relationships with all of these individuals because a cohesive multi-agency approach is the only way to ensure the holistic and personalised education that every pupil deserves.

In light of the Children and Families Act 2014 and the subsequent *Code of Practice: 0–25 Years* (DfE, 2014a), LAs are obliged to publish a local offer which is usually on their website. This provides information regarding provision they expect to be available across education, health and social care for children and young people in their area who have any level of SEND.

 Key points to remember

- Every specialist setting is unique, continuously developing and extending the professionals they will be working with.
- Job titles vary across different contexts and local authorities. You need to find out the varying roles in the provision you are working in.
- The support staff have a critical role, as teaching in specialist provision would be impossible without them, so value them and their contribution.
- The LA must publish a local offer outlining provision available across the services of education, health and care.

Additional resources

As well as the resources you'll find at **www.sagepub.co.uk/martindenham** you should also take a look at the following:

Department for Education (DfE) (2011a) *Teachers' Standards*. London: DfE. These teaching standards define the minimum level of practice expected of trainee and practising teachers in England.

Department for Education (DfE) (2014a) *Special Educational Needs and Disability Code of Practice: 0–25 Years*. London: DfE. This is essential reading. Section 3, 'Working together across education, health and care for joint outcomes' relates particularly well to this chapter and provides detailed outlines of the roles and responsibilities of staff involved in the care and education of children and young people.

The NHS website www.nhscareers.nhs.uk/a-to-z/#S provides an outline, including video clips of the roles and responsibilities of a range of health professions such as SLT, music therapist, paediatrician and school nurse.

CHAPTER 3

YOUR FIRST DAY IN SPECIALIST PROVISION

Dawn Henderson and Sarah Martin-Denham

Key ideas explored in this chapter

- How to prepare for your first day in a specialist context
- What to wear and why
- What to expect on your first day in school
- How to communicate effectively with pupils with a range of needs
- How to manage over-familiar or challenging behaviour and pupils in distress

---

There are a variety of different types of special educational provision depending on the requirements of each geographical area. These may include specialist schools, primary and secondary including post 16, pupil referral units, hubs, nurture units and specialist units attached to schools.

How to prepare for your first day in a specialist context

This may be your first experience of being in a specialist context and like any new provision you may have a range of feelings and emotions. You can prepare for your visit by exploring the school website, which will give you a feel for the particular needs of the pupils, their age range and the type and size of provision. The most recent Office for Standards in Education (Ofsted) report will also give you an understanding of the strengths of the school.

The personal identification you will need to enter the provision will also vary between LAs. You must always have your Disclosure and Barring Service (DBS) check with you and some form of photographic identification. Some schools will also require one other form of identification (ID), so it is worth confirming in advance what you need to take.

 Key points to remember

- Find out who is your point of contact for the school and as a matter of professional courtesy ring to introduce yourself.
- Clarify the identification you need to take with you to the school.
- Find out what time it is convenient for you to arrive and who you should ask for.
- Ask the school if they would like you to send anything in advance to prepare the pupils for your arrival. For example, if you are going to be working with pupils with autism it might be necessary to email your photograph in advance.

What to wear and why

On your first day arrive dressed appropriately to the advice that you have been given by the school. On subsequent days wear clothing that reflects the context that you are in.

 Key points to remember

- Be aware that some clothing can put you in a vulnerable position, for example low-cut/high-rise tops, short skirts and tight trousers.
- Keep jewellery to a minimum as some pupils may become distracted by bright, colourful, dangly jewellery and try to remove it from you.

- Don't wear overpowering perfume or aftershave as this may unsettle those with sensory sensitivities.
- Tie long hair back to avoid tempting pupils to get hold and pull it.
- Wear flat shoes so that you are comfortable and can move quickly and safely.
- Be aware that wearing a school identification can be a source of risk as they can be grabbed by pupils, particularly identification on a lanyard.

What to expect on your first day in school

Schools should have an induction programme in place to familiarise you with their systems. This may include a health and safety briefing, an overview of policies, protocols, the day-to-day running of the school and meeting the staff. You must find out who the Designation Officer is for safeguarding so you know who to go to should a pupil make a disclosure to you or you have any concerns regarding a pupil's wellbeing.

? Key questions to consider

- Who is your first line of contact during your time in school?
- What are the school's expectations of you in terms of professional conduct and daily responsibilities?
- Where can you access information about routines, policies and procedures including safeguarding and who the designated officer (DO) is?
- What are the particular needs of the pupils in your class/school including individual targets, abilities, interests and any triggers for behaviours?
- Are there any pupils in the class who will be particularly anxious about your presence?
- Are there any individual care or medical needs you need to be aware of?
- What are the roles and responsibilities of other adults in the classroom?

CASE STUDY

A reflection on a first day in a specialist context

Emma Phillips: Secondary Professional Year, University of Sunderland
Science with Biology Specialism

On my first day in a specialist secondary school I met my School Based Trainer and had a tour of the school. I was introduced to the staff and I was informed about their particular roles and responsibilities. I was surprised by the range of needs accommodated by one school. By the end of the day I was tired as I had received a lot of new information, but as the days went on I began to digest everything and I realised there was no such thing as a stupid question. The relationships you can build with pupils in a specialist school are immense compared to my experiences in mainstream. This may be due to class sizes being smaller and your greater understanding of the particular needs of the pupils. The placement has broadened my knowledge in terms of the varying needs of pupils and made me think about issues I wouldn't have considered without this experience.

How to communicate effectively with pupils with a range of needs

Depending on the individual context of the school you may encounter pupils with a vast range of levels of communication. There will be some pupils who will have difficulty with articulating themselves due to their specific needs and others who have exceptional communication skills. It is important that you familiarise yourself with individual needs and the level of engagement of the pupils you are working with as early as possible. You need to be aware that the strategies that may be appropriate in one setting may not apply to other settings, for example a pupil referral unit (PRU).

Communication strategies

When working with pupils of secondary/post 16 ages you need to be aware that their level of engagement may be similar to that of a much younger child. Therefore consideration should be given to both the level of language you use and the body language associated with your interactions with the pupil: for example, ensuring you are at the pupil's eye level and you are aware of personal space in your approach.

 Reflective activity

You have been allocated teaching responsibility for a post 16 group who have complex additional needs. One pupil has produced a particularly good drawing during an art class. How would you introduce yourself and engage the pupil to interact with you? How would you ensure that your communication skills are effective?

 Key points to remember

- Use language appropriate for pupils' developmental stage.
- Use the expertise of staff to build up a picture of the individual pupils to support your interactions. For example, what are the pupil's interests, dislikes and needs?
- Be aware that some pupils may have processing impairment and in such cases ensure that your sentences are concise and that adequate time is given for responses.
- Ensure that you provide sufficient personal space (arm's length).

As is the case with most classrooms, there may be times when you witness and have to deal with new behaviours. The following section has been included to provide you with additional guidance should you need to draw upon it.

How to manage over-familiar or challenging behaviour and pupils in distress

Hopefully, during your induction the school will have discussed potential situations that may arise and how to deal with them. If not, the following strategies may be useful in immediately addressing problematic situations. It is important to note that pupils display behaviours for a reason, and the staff will be able to support you once they are aware that you feel uncomfortable.

For pupils who are over-familiar or in distress

- Ask members of the school staff what you should do/how you should respond.
- Use opportunities to observe the strategies used by other members of the school team. You could replicate those same strategies with the pupil.

Challenging behaviour

It is essential that you are aware of the individual 'behaviour policy' in which you are working. This policy will give detailed guidance on the range of interventions used when managing different levels of challenging behaviour. Schools may have additional policies relating to positive handling.

It is important to understand that any physical intervention is carefully planned and is carried out by trained staff, in the best interests of the pupil. On the occasion that you observe a planned physical intervention it may appear distressing for the pupil involved and leave you feeling unsettled. It is vital that following the event you have an opportunity to debrief. If you are in a position as trainee teacher your training provider will also give you with support.

 Reflective activity

It is your first day in a specialist context working with primary age pupils with autism. During assembly one of the pupils approached you and grabbed your hair. The pupil would not release your hair from her grip.
   Consider your reaction to this situation:

How should you respond?
How could you prevent the situation happening again?

The outcome

A TA became aware of what was happening and came to the teacher's aid. He held the pupil's hand until the pupil was encouraged to let go. Through a debrief with the school the teacher learned that

> the pupil likes the texture of hair and the best reaction is to respond by putting your hand over the pupil's to prevent them pulling. This taught the trainee teacher the importance of understanding the reason for the behaviour and thinking before reacting. The pupil did not want to cause pain and it was not intended to be a personal attack. It is advisable to tie your hair back when working in a specialist context.

Other unique behaviours

There are a range of behaviours which may be demonstrated that can be indicators to a pupil's state of wellbeing. These may range from finger picking or hair twiddling through to more extreme behaviours of self-harming. However, much behaviour a pupil displays is simply a form of self-regulation and is part of their daily routine.

Pupils with additional medical needs

A number of pupils may have complex and additional medical needs that may include the requirement of equipment such as feeds, pumps or other supportive devices. It could be that the pupils you are working with are on several medications. The medication will often have side-effects that will have an impact on their ability to engage with you, so don't take it personally if they fall asleep.

Side-effects of medication or illness can cause pupils to:

- feel very tired and in some cases fall asleep;
- be physically sick or feel nauseous;
- be lethargic;
- have mood swings;
- display negative behaviours such as hitting out or appearing agitated.

The best advice is to show an interest and find out what you can about the individual pupils. The information will prepare you for how the pupils may present and respond in different situations. You could find out this information from the class teacher, the SENCO, a member of the support staff or if appropriate the parents/carers.

Teacher health and wellbeing

In all of this it is important to consider that in a new and specialist setting you may come away from your first day with mixed emotions. To have the opportunity to work with pupils in a specialist context is a privilege. Teaching in any setting can at times be challenging, but with that comes an abundance of rewards. From this point and throughout your time within a special educational provision remember to monitor your own health and wellbeing. You can do this by talking through your feelings and emotions with the colleagues you are working with or family and friends.

Additional resources

As well as the resources you'll find at **www.sagepub.co.uk/martindenham** you should also take a look at the following:

Contact a Family, www.cafamily.org.uk/: This website is an extensive source of information. It is useful if you need to find out about the particular aspects of a diagnosed condition such as prevalence, inheritance patterns, treatment, symptoms and for signposting to charities and further information.

Teen Mental Health, www.teenmentalhealth.org/understanding-mental-health/mental-disorders/: This is an American website which explores the challenges pupils with mental health difficulties may encounter. It offers practical advice and free downloadable resources.

CHAPTER 4

TEACHING AND LEARNING

Judith Donovan, Dawn Henderson,
Pauline James and Sarah Martin-Denham

Key ideas explored in this chapter

- Effective learning environments and classroom organisation
- Pupil profiles
- Teaching and learning strategies
- Ways to develop pupil self-worth and self-esteem
- Linking lesson objectives to learning frameworks
- Understanding the importance of removing barriers to learning
- Providing stimulating lessons with multi-sensory approaches
- The importance of teacher modelling and repetition
- Effective questioning techniques
- Developing teacher presence and effective use of the voice
- Learning in and around the school
- The specific needs of pupils with English as an additional language (EAL)

As teachers in any context you are responsible and accountable for the progress and development of those you teach and the effectiveness of the support staff that you deploy. As the teacher you will need to produce inclusive high-quality teaching which is differentiated to cater for the needs, abilities and strengths of the pupils in your class. You will need to be astutely aware of the gaps in the pupils' learning, the barriers to learning they face and their learning preferences before teaching your first class. This chapter will explore effective learning environments and outline how classroom organisation is an essential aspect of ensuring that outstanding teaching and quality learning takes place.

Effective learning environments and classroom organisation

As part of your induction it is crucial that time is spent familiarising yourself with the range of teaching styles and learning strategies in use around the school to ensure that all pupils are challenged, enabling them to meet their full potential through a broad and balanced curriculum. It is useful to shadow a group of pupils over a period of time or observe teaching in a variety of classrooms/age phases, focussing on routines and structures that already exist for the groups. It is vital that these strategies and routines are maintained in the classroom in which you are teaching to prevent the pupils becoming anxious or distressed. Some pupils may have very particular preferences to engage them in the learning process, so you need to be aware of these to promote participation.

When considering your own classroom management and organisation, ensure that that the following are in place:

- Welcome each pupil into the classroom at the start of each session.
- Considering the information that you have about individual pupils, ensure that they are appropriately grouped and accommodated within the classroom environment.
- Use systems already in place to seat pupils, such as picture/name card systems and visual timetables to share the structure of the day.
- Some pupils may need support to remain seated during the lesson, for example they may require foot supports, fiddle toys or simply constant reassurance.
- Work with other members of the team to ensure that pupils are ready to engage in learning and know what is required from them at the beginning of the lesson.
- Ensure that additional adults supporting the group are very clear about the learning outcomes for the session and are effectively deployed to support and assess learning and progress.

- Position yourself so you have a good view of all pupils at all times and carefully use classroom systems in place to support transitions during the lesson.
- Have all resources prepared, ready and at hand before the start of the teaching session.
- Use a wide range of teaching strategies to enable pupils to engage with the learning on offer.
- Ensure that the learning environment and resources you use reflect the diverse society in which we live; use images to highlight the sameness of different children and ensure that images are non-stereotypical, representing both genders in a range of roles.

As pupils get older, hormones and puberty may impact on your seating arrangements and affect which pupils are able to be near each other. The case study below explores the challenges of supporting pupils who are unable to articulate how they are feeling and suggests useful strategies.

CASE STUDY

The challenges of puberty

Alberto was 18 years old with moderate learning difficulties and autism. He struggled to understand and accept that he was no longer a young boy, and preferred to have all decisions made for him. His language and behaviour were inappropriate and, while he fiercely disliked being touched, he would often reach out and stroke others. He was socially isolated and spent much of his time living in a world inside his head where he was seven years of age. Alberto was starting to feel an attraction for another pupil in the class but didn't know how to deal with those feelings. This resulted in aggressive behaviour towards staff and himself, where he would hit the table with his fist and throw chairs. Staff worked with Alberto using a Social Story™ about being a young man and taking responsibility for his own actions. He was also given a key fob attached to his belt with a variety of words and symbols which he could use to share his emotions. Alberto had access to a quiet room where he could go when he started to feel anxious. He was allowed to leave the classroom by showing his 'upset' card and was followed by a favoured member of staff who he could talk to if he wished to.

Pupil profiles

In preparation for teaching pupils with special educational needs and/or disabilities and following your induction it is vitally important that you are pro-active in establishing how the pupils learn, attainment profile, strengths, development needs and any identified needs they have. They will all differ in their individual abilities and social interaction.

To support your planning it is useful to have a brief class/individual pupil overview. This will be useful for any new adults visiting you in school and will allow them to gain an insight into the particular needs of the pupils you are teaching. This may already be available from the class teacher but if not, here is an example of what you may need to consider:

Age: 6 years

Likes: Whiteboard, computer, LEGO and cars

Dislikes: The word 'no', being bumped into and new faces

Communication: Can seem a bit shy and is easily distracted by others

Language: First language Urdu, second language English (Mother speaks Urdu only)

Physical needs: Co-ordination (falls often) and personal care requires support (toileting)

Disabilities: PDA (Pathological Demand Avoidance) Global Delay and wears glasses

Behaviour: Due to his PDA if told 'no' he can become very distressed, he will ignore any demands you make so alternatives need to be used, e.g. 'How could we do this?' rather than 'This is how I want you to.'

 Reflective activity

Find out about PDA by going to The National Autistic Society website. Then, given the profile of the pupil above, what do you need to consider in terms of your use of questioning with this pupil?

The Children and Families Act 2014 places a duty on providers to make arrangements to support pupils with medical conditions through individual healthcare plans. These include their particular needs, how they will be cared for and who will provide the medical support. It is important you are aware of these as using a consistent approach is essential. These plans exist to ensure that all adults working with these pupils follow the same strategies for their individual care. The information can be used to inform other adults and visitors to the classroom of the individual needs of the class.

Teaching and learning strategies

The outline of teaching and learning strategies in this section needs to be used flexibly and assessed for effectiveness against the range of individual learning needs within the context.

Observation is an essential tool to allow you to identify specific areas of progress and development. It enables you to develop your understanding of how effective the learning environment is in terms of meeting the pupils' needs and in promoting independence. Through observation you can also reflect upon the current provision, how effective the routines are, how pupils are responding to different teaching strategies and how effective the range of interactions are, such as pupil to pupil, pupil to adult and adult to adult. The role of observation cannot be overestimated in planning for teaching and learning.

Sharing instructions with pupils with SEN requires careful consideration. Some pupils have difficulty processing complex sentences so it is important to keep language simple and necessary. For example, 'Hello Jack, check your timetable' could be more appropriately worded as 'Jack, check timetable'. You then need to repeat the instruction to remind the pupil what it is you need them to do. This supports the individual who may only remember the final words spoken in a longer sentence.

Appropriate and open body language is important when establishing a positive teacher–pupil relationship. You need to use non-verbal communication to aid your interactions with the pupils you are teaching. Consider your facial expressions, posture, gesturing, use of eye contact and voice tones. Does your non-verbal communication reflect your interest and enthusiasm for teaching? It is important that you provide a learning environment that fosters mutual respect, commitment to learning, enthusiasm and participation. Where there is a strong partnership pupils are comfortable in taking risks and assuming control of their own learning. How you present yourself to pupils will also have an immense impact on how they respond to you and the world around them.

The use of supportive language will motivate the pupils and improve their self-esteem. Using phrases such as 'I know you can do it' and 'Can you show me what you can do?' will encourage pupil participation. There will be instances where pupils lack the confidence to complete the activities. In these situations you need to find a way to facilitate the learning by identifying the barrier to learning. You could ask 'What can I do to help you?' If a pupil is facing challenges, your choice of language can impact on their self-worth. You must always find a way to allow the pupil to participate and succeed. Remember, it is not just the language you use but also your facial expressions. If you are frowning or raising your eyebrows whilst saying something positive the pupil will receive mixed messages about what you mean.

Within your classroom organisation you need to consider how you will group the pupils. Pupils can be grouped by ability, pairs, subject, friendships, role models (e.g. those efficient with the use of symbols to those who are new to the system). Group work holds many benefits such as learning to listen, wait and turn take, and being able to communicate to an audience and make choices. Being part of a group will also improve the pupil's self-esteem as successes are celebrated together. Collaborative learning will give opportunities for pupils to 'think, pair and share', and is particularly suited to mixed-ability working. The groupings need to allow for access to adult support and should be based on those working on similar learning objectives.

The structure of the teaching session needs to be carefully considered. The use of a visual timetable will support you in preparing the pupils for your lessons. You will need to decide how you are going to share the learning objectives and outline prior learning. It is advisable to ask the class teacher what works best in the class you are in. You also will need strategies to signal the beginning and end of group work such as playing music or singing a song, then consistently use the same approach. Ensure that you have all resources and equipment ready and at hand and check that any technology is working and set up in advance of the lesson. You need to have a plan B should the activity be unsuccessful to bring the group back together. Consider using a motivator such as food and reward systems to encourage pupil participation. Remember to include clear differentiation based upon the individual needs of the pupils you are teaching and share this information with the other adults.

Key points to remember

- Find out the prior learning for you to build upon and ensure that you know the particular needs, abilities and strengths of the pupils you are teaching.
- Ensure that all support staff are clearly briefed in terms of the learning objectives for the pupils they are working with.
- Many pupils will respond to singing better than speech.
- Always begin with the pupil's name when speaking to them so that they know it is them you are talking to.
- Use simple and only necessary language.
- Show that you are listening by maintaining appropriate eye contact and giving acknowledgement through nodding.
- Give pupils time to communicate as some individuals require additional thinking and response time.
- Have supportive strategies in place so that pupils can communicate their needs/wants; for example, PECS®, signing systems such as Makaton® and British Sign Language (BSL).

It is important that within your role you are promoting pupil involvement and active participation in learning. There must be the use of practical, kinaesthetic/audio visual approaches in all lessons including sensory (haptic touch) to ensure that all learning preferences are catered for. You should also be planning to teach some of your sessions in the outdoor environment. The pupils should have a say in what they are going to learn and how this will happen. They will all have individual targets which you will support them in working towards.

? **Key questions to consider**

- Am I knowledgeable about the individual targets and access requirements for the pupils I am going to teach?
- Have I provided opportunities for the pupils to record in a variety of media such as audio, video, photographs, online mind mapping and written methods?
- Have the pupils had a say in what they are going to learn and how?
- Have I discussed with the support staff what they learned and what their next steps are going to be?

CASE STUDY

Building self-esteem

Anna was six and an elective mute with SLD. When she first started school, at the age of four, she would not speak. She would nod and give eye contact to staff and peers, but would not make a sound. While at home, Anna communicated freely and would even shout and squeal. In school, Anna was encouraged to speak by carefully building her self-esteem through small steps of progress and extensive praise. Once a relationship had been established with particular members of staff and Anna felt comfortable in school, they began to encourage her to at least make a sound before she was given what she was asking for. She had 'yes' and 'no' cards which staff insisted that she use (instead of pointing or nodding), and was then taught how to use symbols in order to facilitate her communication. In time, during a soft play session with two special friends, and a particular member of staff, Anna began to laugh, squeak and shout a few words. Staff reproduced this same learning environment across other subjects and with other activities. Anna began to speak consistently, if very quietly, with one member of staff. In order to encourage a louder voice staff would initiate a variety of hide and seek games where Anna had to tell the group she was ready, and they would respond 'We can't hear you'. Anna really enjoyed this, and her voice would become louder and louder. By very gradually withdrawing this favoured member of staff, it was hoped that Anna would speak to other members of the team.

Ways to develop pupil self-worth and self-esteem

There are several ways in which teachers can encourage pupils to develop self-worth and self-esteem, for example to:

- define rules and expectations clearly;
- create opportunities for positive communication and value the interaction;
- tune in to anxieties and know what their triggers are;
- recognise effort as well as achievement so they know that what they do is important to you;
- consistently use praise, celebrating successes and achievements;
- tell them 'why' what they have produced is good;
- create opportunities for independent actions and share their success.

Reflective activity

What other ways can you think of to develop the self-belief of an individual pupil of your choice? Who do you need to work with to achieve this?

Linking lesson objectives to learning frameworks

In preparation for learning you will need to find out the framework that the school or department is using to set objectives. Schools may use the EYFS framework (DfE 2014b), performance indicators for value added target setting (PIVATS), or the primary and secondary National Curriculum (NC) schemes of work (SoW) from Entitlement and Quality Education for Pupils with Learning Difficulties (EQUALS) or the schools' own developed SoW.

Learning objectives should be clearly linked to the framework in use and should be age appropriate, achievable, measurable, relevant and meaningful to both the pupil and the other adults within the classroom. You will need to ensure that the curriculum is differentiated to appropriate teaching objectives for the individual pupils you teach. This means that you may have seven pupils in your class and your lesson is differentiated in seven ways to meet their individual needs and abilities. This will be discussed further in Chapter 12.

Understanding the importance of removing barriers to learning

Learning and progress can be negatively impacted on if the teacher is unaware of the individual barriers to learning within their classroom. These barriers may be seen or unseen, from specific behavioural difficulties to noise and light levels within the classroom. For those pupils with SEN and complex difficulties, changing one facet of the classroom such as moving furniture or changing a display can cause anxiety and distress.

In all specialist schools each pupil will have individual targets and usually an EHC plan. These plans should include targets for pupils focussing on their particular barriers to learning. Understanding the challenges for the pupils in your class will support your planning, enabling you to deliver differentiated lessons which will hopefully include strategies to support your pupils to reach their full potential.

Key questions to consider

- How can I incorporate the interests and learning preferences of the pupils into my teaching?
- How can I ensure that the family are involved in the learning process?
- How can I find out the specific barriers to learning for the individual pupils and what can I do to remove them when I am in school?

CASE STUDY

The importance of consistency in managing behaviours

Laura, aged nine, is a pupil in Key Stage 2 who has SLD and exhibits severe challenging behaviour. In a classroom situation she finds ordinary day-to-day interactions too stimulating, and so can be disruptive and aggressive towards other pupils and staff, hitting out, biting and spitting. In order to make her behaviour more manageable a reward chart was introduced where she worked towards getting three 'cat' stickers in order to have her choice of activity. This was linked to the use of a visual timetable to structure Laura's day, and access to a quiet area where she could work with one-to-one support when necessary.

A consistent approach was used by all staff (including her home-to-school taxi escort) as Laura would look for weaknesses in management to try to manipulate the situation, usually to avoid work. Typically, Laura would be met from her home-to-school transport and would be immediately engaged in conversation, using key words and short sentences, about which reward she will choose today, how she would achieve it, and how pleased everyone would be. Once she was in the classroom Laura would be given visual reminders in the use of her timetable, reward card, and a picture of who would be working with her to help her gain her rewards. Throughout the day this was reinforced in the same way, with constant small-step support, modelling of the required behaviour, a quiet environment, a non-confrontational manner, consistent eye contact, and co-counting to 20 slowly once she started to get upset. At the end of the day Laura was given a sticker to put in her home-school diary to show her mother that she had had a good day.

Providing stimulating lessons with multi-sensoᵣ

It is likely that lessons within a specialist setting may take a ⌐
form to those in a mainstream school. Lessons may differ ⌐
require short bursts of activity between learning episodes anⅬ
incorporate sessions of therapeutic input from other professionals.

In a specialist context it is crucial to provide a calm and constanⅬ
environment which is conducive to teaching and learning. However,
in reality there are often many interruptions of which the majority
will be essential, such as pupils being withdrawn for therapies.

Within a specialist context you will see the importance and impact
of providing a multi-sensory approach to teaching and learning.
Effective lessons are those which engage all the five senses of sight,
smell, sound, taste and hearing. A key skill is to be able to identify and act upon the different learning preferences of the individual
pupil. Some pupils may require exaggerated gesture, expression and
objects of reference (visual supports) to engage them fully, whereas
others may respond to a low-stimulus approach.

 Reflective activity

Identify the multi-sensory teaching approaches that could be used
when reading the story *Jack and the Beanstalk*. (Some suggestions are
given at the end of the chapter.)

The importance of teacher modelling and repetition

Modelling is a fundamental means by which pupils with special
educational needs and/or disabilities learn. The use of demonstration
to show the process and end product of an activity before asking
them to do it is an essential method of teaching. By the teacher
using kinaesthetic and visual approaches, pupils will learn through
observation what is required of them. For pupils with SEN verbal
explanation can often be very challenging, particularly because, as
reflected earlier, they may only remember the final words of a sentence or instruction. In a specialist context it is more likely that
pupils will experience challenges in retaining information. In light of
this it is essential that a small-steps approach is used to provide
pupils with opportunities to practise skills through repetition.

Effective questioning techniques

How you question pupils in a specialist context will vary depending on their individual needs. You will need to consider how you will use questions to determine what the pupils know and understand; you will need this information to inform your planning. When asking questions you need to ensure that you give appropriate response time as some pupils may need longer to process the question. Keep the question clear and concise and begin it with the pupil's name. How you ask a question will vary in terms of its complexity depending on the needs of the individual pupils.

Developing teacher presence and effective use of the voice

There is much discussion about teacher presence and what this is. A teacher without this may come across as uninterested or detached. As a teacher you need to be a performer and in that role engage all the pupils that you teach. It is vital to utilise all the teaching strategies that you gain to create an enthusiastic and engaging environment, which could include the use of props, alternative voices, role play and/ or technology.

In a classroom and lesson setting, teacher voice can be a very effective teaching tool. Using a range of voice tones, loudness and projection it is possible to bring a group to quiet or enthuse a group in activity. Effective use of teacher voice alongside exuberant gestures can engage pupils in an activity that would otherwise seem mundane.

If you feel that this is an area that you need to develop, then a useful strategy is to film parts of your teaching to allow you to reflect on how you present. This must only be done with permission from the school.

Key points for effective teacher presence

- Sit or stand up straight.
- Smile and make eye contact with every pupil.
- Use humour.
- Exaggerate your facial expressions.
- Involve the pupils, interacting in a meaningful way.
- Use resources and props that you have to hand to engage the group visually.

- Act confidently with enthusiasm, engagement and pleasure in your teaching.
- Look as though this is the best lesson you are having with the best group you teach!

Learning in and around the school

In specialist and mainstream contexts there is scope for teaching in an alternative environment. Examples of these could be hydrotherapy pools, soft play areas, outdoor growing areas, forest schools, community areas or open spaces. Although some of the settings lend themselves to specialist therapeutic provision, many can be used for teaching cross-curricular skills. For example, using a soft play area to teach recognition of shape in mathematics. As most specialist settings would engage in community learning, this could also be considered as an opportunity to take learning outside of the classroom.

Forest schools are, essentially, about learning from the outdoor environment. Some schools will have their own forest school on site, others may have to be travelled to. All areas of the curriculum can be taught outside, stimulating the imagination and bringing subjects to life in a real context. Pupils could make a shelter or a den as part of work on *Swallows and Amazons* or carve magic wands and cook up campfire cauldron spells related to the *Harry Potter* stories. *The Stickman* story could be used to whittle stick men, exploring the personal, social and health education (PSHE) subjects of friendship, feeling lonely, lost and worried, and exploring what our 'stickmen' would do in different situations. A campfire circle is also very effective for 'circle time' with story telling, singing and developing turn taking and waiting skills. Older pupils can benefit from risk taking and assessing risk for themselves in an ever changing environment, enhancing the lifelong independence living skills of problem solving. Forest school sessions can also help to stimulate communication and language development, prompted by sensory experiences, and develop confidence skills in independence, social skills and disability awareness.

 Reflective activity

Which other areas of the curriculum would benefit from a forest schools approach? Plan a scheme of work or series of lessons incorporating the forest school environment for your chosen age range.

The specific needs of pupils with English as an additional language (EAL)

It is important to reiterate that just because a pupil does not have a good command of English it does not mean they have SEN. It needs to be determined where the difficulties are due to learning English as an additional language (EAL) or whether it is due to an underlying special educational need or disability. There will, of course, be pupils in schools who do have SEN and also have EAL, but they are the minority. You may have a pupil join your class who is 'newly arrived' or a 'beginner in English'. It is important to note that pupils with EAL have recognisable patterns of development which differ from those whose first language is English. This section sets out to provide some strategies to support the teaching of these pupils.

 Key questions to consider

- What are the languages spoken by the family and the pupil?
- What are the educational history and particular needs of the child?
- What is their religion/cultural heritage?
- Who might have further information on the pupil, such as English-speaking relatives, or do you have access to a translator?
- When you have the answers to these questions you need to consider how you will use the information to support the pupil.

 Key points to remember

- Value the pupil's contributions in their native language.
- Get involved with the family so you can develop an understanding of their social, linguistic and cultural lives.
- Celebrate the pupil's heritage and embed it into your teaching and school environment.

Additional resources

As well as the resources you'll find at **www.sagepub.co.uk/martindenham** you should also take a look at the following:

Flo Longhorn has a range of books, blogs and helpful guides to support you in using technology in your everyday teaching. If you search for Flo via the Internet, a range of links will be available for you to explore.

National Association for Language Development in the Curriculum (NALDIC), www.naldic.org.uk/eal-teaching-and-learning/eal-resources/eal-sen: This website provides a range of resources, strategies and research to support those teaching pupils who are both SEN and EAL.

SENICT, www.ianbean.co.uk: Ian Bean's website has a wealth of knowledge and experience in teaching pupils with SEN. In the resources section of the website Ian has a selection of free downloadable guidance information on subjects such as sensory stories, using cameras and iPad apps.

TES iboard, www.iboard.co.uk: This site has many interactive free resources for a range of subjects. The resources are for a range of ages and are easy to use.

Possible solutions

For the Reflective activity on p. 33

- Objects of reference to touch and feel, such as dried beans in an open topped container and a furry cow to pass around for the group to feel and describe.
- Materials of different textures, such as fur for the cow, feathers for the hen and leaves for the plant.
- Enormous shoes to try on to represent the Giant's feet.
- Sounds such as the cow mooing, banging a drum to represent the footsteps. If a very large drum was used the pupils could lie on it and feel the vibrations.
- A water spray for the Giant's sweat or sneezes.
- Grass to smell for the beanstalk.

CHAPTER 5

PLANNING FOR LEARNING

Judith Donovan, Dawn Henderson,
Pauline James and Sarah Martin-Denham

Key ideas explored in this chapter

- Why planning is important
- Approaches to planning
- Elements to include in weekly/daily planning
- Identifying suitable learning objectives and success criteria
- Differentiation to meet all needs and abilities
- Incorporating pupil voice and interests
- Personalised targets and inclusive planning
- Levels of progress using the P scales
- Expected levels of progress for pupils with SEN
- Breaking down learning into small steps over a series of lessons
- Using reflective lesson evaluations to inform future planning
- Preparing pupils for transition readiness

This chapter builds further on Chapter 4, Teaching and Learning. There are examples of planning for a range of ages and contexts in the online extras at www.sage.co.uk/martindenham.

Once you are aware of the individual needs of the pupils you are going to teach and following discussions with the SENCO or other members of the team, you can begin to plan for learning and development. The SENCO and class teacher(s) will be able to tell you which pupils have an EHC plan and which require SEN Support. The school will be able to share with you the outcomes they are seeking, the interventions and support needed for individual pupils and the expected impact on progress and development. You need to use this information when planning for learning and in communication with parents/carers so they can consolidate learning at home.

Why planning is important

When planning in a specialist context it is important to be mindful that you will be planning not only for the learner but also for the additional support that may be in your lesson. The role of support staff within the lesson must be explicit within your lesson plan. Effective deployment of support staff is where the individual takes responsibility for the learning and progress of learners rather than simply facilitating a lesson delivered by the teacher.

Planning is the keystone of a good lesson. Carefully planned and structured lessons are vital to support pupils in their learning. Teachers need to have a clear and well thought through idea of what it is they are intending to teach and how they are going to teach it. This must be stated plainly through the learning objective and lesson plan outline and reflect individual needs with a clear understanding of what the outcome will be for each pupil.

Approaches to planning

There are three levels of planning, long, medium and short-term. In general, a long-term plan (LTP) would outline an overview of the learning that will take place over a long period of time to ensure that there is no repetition and that resources are widely available. It ensures that children are learning appropriately to their chronological and developmental stage/age with themes that interest and inspire them. All schools plan in different ways and the definitions of long, medium and short-term planning are very fluid. Long-term planning is ultimately led by the National Frameworks.

It is essential that you familiarise yourself with the approaches to planning that your individual school has in place and be aware of how long, medium and short-term planning link together. Some schools link medium-term planning (MTP) directly to individual lesson plans, whereas others may use weekly planning to support daily/short-term planning (STP).

The key elements of an effective medium-term plan are that it:

- is structured week by week – usually daily in the EYFS (DfE, 2014a) – showing progression in learning, in a grid format for ease of use;
- shows prior learning – what the pupil has learned in terms of the subject in previous years/lessons;
- includes key skills and areas of learning and what knowledge, understanding and skills are to be developed;
- includes clear learning objectives and success criteria;
- links directly to the National Frameworks;
- includes cross-curricular links where appropriate, teaching and learning strategies, resources, differentiated activities and assessment approaches;
- is produced in consultation with the pupils.

The weekly/daily planning will be derived from the LTP and MTP. The planning needs to show how you are promoting independence and how you have considered the pupil's aspirations, interests, needs, gaps in learning and any barriers to learning that they face. Once you have this information you can begin to plan for high-quality teaching.

Elements to include in weekly/daily planning

There are several elements that must be included in weekly or daily planning, such as:

- Clear differentiation in consideration of individual needs and abilities.
- An outline of pupil groupings: ability, friendship and interests.
- Precise learning outcomes.
- A detailed outline of who the support staff will be teaching and what they will be teaching.
- Descriptive activity outlines with an introduction, main activity and a plenary, with timings.
- Resources clearly listed.
- Identification of opportunities for cross-curricular links.

- Opportunities for pupils' voice highlighted.
- Potential misconceptions identified.
- Prior learning, what they know so far.
- Key vocabulary to be discussed.
- Key questions you will ask and who you will target them towards.
- Specific supportive strategies for pupils with SEN/EAL/higher ability.
- Behaviour management strategies for specific pupils.
- Assessment opportunities/target pupils.
- Evaluation of learning and next steps.

Identifying suitable learning objectives and success criteria

Ensuring that you have appropriate learning objectives and success criteria is essential to an effective lesson. They are there to keep the teacher on track with what they are teaching, to ensure that the pupils know exactly what is expected of them and to guide the other support staff in the class.

Learning objectives and success criteria need to be:

- age appropriate, specific, measurable, relevant, understandable, achievable and challenging;
- well thought through;
- in small steps, knowing what comes next and what has gone before;
- shared with the pupils in a way they can access.

 Key points to remember

- Every pupil needs to be catered for during the lesson. They may need objects of reference (visual supports), communication aids, symbols, to be positioned comfortably and to have the correct sized desk and chair.
- A clear understanding of communication systems used is essential. Think before the lesson about what is needed, for example if Makaton® is used check that the symbols and signs are known and available for key words.
- Always consider the appropriateness of resources. Will they grab the pupils' interest and motivate them and are they age appropriate?
- Ensure that you include enough time for repetition/reinforcement of learning.

Differentiation to meet all needs and abilities

You need to show on your planning how you are meeting the needs of all pupils. Once you know the individual pupils' skills and abilities you can then begin to find ways for them to access the next steps of learning. It may be that you differentiate by ability, so plan according to their current attainment levels or sublevels. You may have the same learning objective but the pupils' tasks may be different or they may record the activity in a different way.

You need to consider the access strategies, how you ensure that the pupils can access what you are teaching them. This should be indicated clearly on your weekly/daily lesson plans.

？ Key questions to consider

- Do I need a range of paper sizes, coloured overlays or enlarged print?
- Have I included alternative ways of recording work which do not involve the written word, such as mind mapping, touch screen devices, audio recordings, images and labelling?
- Have I broken the learning into small achievable steps?
- Have I ensured that each pupil has an appropriate level of challenge?
- Am I building on prior learning and am I responsive to the pupil's needs and wishes?

The process of planning targeted provision for a pupil with an EHC plan needs to be well considered. As the needs of these pupils are complex, the approach to meeting these needs must be both personalised and individually targeted. The planning and teaching must be rooted in the planned outcomes in their EHC plan. The case study below demonstrates how differentiation by learning preference can make a difference to pupil engagement and achievement.

CASE STUDY

Personalising learning through differentiation

Ashleigh was a trainee teacher in the third year of her degree. She was on her teaching practice in a specialist context which predominantly catered for primary aged pupils with autism. She was teaching seven pupils aged eight to nine years and was able to use signing to communicate effectively with the pupils. Ashleigh was due to be observed and was unsure how to differentiate effectively for her class. The lesson she planned had one overall objective but was differentiated seven ways for the seven pupils. The lesson plan outlined the particular needs of individual pupils, their strengths, anxieties, triggers and motivators (food in this case). The pupils were organising foods into healthy and unhealthy categories. The planning for the support staff was clear and they all knew the learning objective and had resources and recording methods to suit their pupils. For example, one pupil sorted into hoops, another took photographs (as he was passionate about technology) and another made a healthy sandwich. The lesson was observed by an Ofsted inspector and Ashleigh was graded outstanding due to her ability to personalise the learning to allow the pupils to achieve their best.

Incorporating pupil voice and interests

It is important that you get to know your class well before you can begin to plan for their learning. Prior to planning any sessions make sure you have had discussions with the class teacher about the individual needs and interests of the pupils and what motivates them. Read any information available about each pupil. You need to know which of the four broad areas of need and support the pupils' difficulties fall into: communication and interaction; cognition and learning; social, emotional and mental health; and sensory and/or physical needs (DfE, 2014b). Knowing this information will give you an overview of their needs and how to plan for them. Of course, there will be pupils who have needs in all of the broad areas and these may change over time. Many schools have pen portraits/passports or information sheets about the pupils in each class. These are important to your success; discover what the pupils like, respond to or dislike and what makes them anxious.

? Key questions to consider

- Do the pupils I am going to teach have targets set for speech and language development, occupational therapy, physiotherapy or behaviour support plans?
- How can I find out this information so that I can begin planning for learning?

All this information will create a picture of the pupils for whom you are going to plan. You need to have a secure understanding of how well your pupils communicate and how you will support them to let you know what they have understood. The Assessment for Learning (AfL) section in Chapter 6 further explores some ideas on how pupils can communicate their views on their achievements.

Personalised targets and inclusive planning

Often, in a special educational provision, each pupil has an individual learning package through which their needs are met. The setting of personalised pupil targets is intended to address specific and individual SEN of those pupils. The targets may be focussed on their academic, behavioural, social or basic skills and these must be deliberately ambitious. No two pupils are the same in their learning needs, or in how they respond to being taught. Each pupil will be following their own targets, and these need to be included in your weekly/daily planning. The targets may be typical learning outcomes, but they may also involve how to sit, or how to share with other pupils. The whole team needs to be aware of these targets and share information on the pupils' progress towards them.

Levels of progress using the P scales

P scales were introduced for pupils with SEN over five years of age who were working below level 1 of the National Curriculum (NC) and have recently been updated (DfE, 2014c). The P scales break down subjects into small achievable steps highlighting the important skills, knowledge and understanding a pupil needs before moving on to work at NC level 1. They are available for Art and Design, Design and Technology, English (reading, writing, speaking and listening), Geography, History, Computing, Mathematics (using and applying mathematics, number, shape, space and measures), Languages, Music, Physical Education, PSHE and Citizenship, Religious Education and Science.

P scales explained

The P scale is broken down from P1 at the lowest through to P8 which is often termed as working towards NC level 1.

P1 to P3 are for the earliest levels of attainment and are common across English, Mathematics and Science. The levels outline the types and range of general performance that some pupils with learning difficulties might characteristically demonstrate. The three levels P1 to P3 are further split into sublevels (i) and (ii). For example, in English (speaking/expressive communication):

At the lowest level **P1(i):**

'Pupils encounter activities and experiences. They may be passive or resistant. They may show simple reflex responses, any participation is fully prompted.'

At **P3(ii)**:

'Pupils use emerging conventional communication. They greet known people and may initiate interactions and activities. They can remember learned responses over increasing periods of time and may anticipate known events. They may respond to options and choices with actions or gestures. They actively explore objects and events for more extended periods. They apply potential solutions systematically to problems.'

P4 to P8 show subject-related attainment. In the case of English (listening) the P levels descriptor increases in challenge as the level progresses.

P4 Pupils demonstrate an understanding of at least 50 words, including the names of familiar objects. Pupils respond appropriately to simple requests which contain one key word, sign or symbol in familiar situations; for example, 'Get your coat', 'Stand up' or 'Clap your hands'.

Through to:

P8 Pupils take part in role play with confidence. Pupils listen attentively. They respond appropriately to questions about why or how; for example, 'Why does a bird make a nest?', 'How do we copy this picture?'.

PIVATS

To support the assessment of progress, each P level is broken down into five smaller steps which are recorded (e, d, c, b, a). These five steps indicate whether a pupil is:

Just beginning to achieve within that particular P level = Level P4e

or

A pupil is working securely within that particular P level = Level P4a

For a pupil working within the range P1 to P3, this includes the sublevels indicated earlier. So a pupil working securely at P3(i) would be recorded as P3(i)a.

In schools where pupils may have severe and complex learning difficulty the PIVATS system is also used to facilitate even smaller steps assessment. PIVATS stands for: **P**erformance **I**ndicators **V**alue

Added Target Setting. PIVATS further breaks down both the P levels and NC levels into five more reduced steps. By the time you come to work and assess pupils with severe and complex learning difficulties, the value of PIVATS will be clear.

Why are P levels and PIVATS useful?

- For showing a pupil's strengths.
- To show progress in small steps.
- To help professionals describe progress in a consistent way.

It is important at this point to acknowledge that in June 2013 the Department for Education announced that the system of NC levels would be removed because it believed the system was difficult for parents to understand. The majority of primary and secondary schools may still continue with the NC levels as a method of assessment and reporting.

Expected levels of progress for pupils with SEN

One of the key principles of the Department for Education progression guidance document (DfE, 2010) was for there to be high expectations for all learners identified as having SEND. The progression guidance sets out a clear national expectation of the minimum rate of progress that 'all pupils' of 'all abilities' should make: two NC levels of progress between Key Stage 1 and Key Stage 2 and three NC levels of progress between Key Stage 3 and Key Stage 4. This is particularly challenging in a specialist setting.

Table 5.1 shows the relative working range of an 11-year-old pupil with learning difficulties in comparison with national averages.

  Reflective activity

Consider that an average 11-year-old would be working at NC level 4 in a mainstream setting. Your class may have pupils with SLD and be working at an average level of P7. How would you plan individual challenge into your lesson to ensure that all learners meet the expectation of three levels of progress by the end of Key Stage 4? (Some suggestions are given at the end of the chapter.)

Table 5.1 Expected levels of progress by age

level	National averages	11-year-olds with learning difficulties
P1		Pupils working within this range of levels usually have Profound and multiple difficulties (PMLD)
P2		
P3		
P4		
P5		Pupils working within this range of levels usually have Severe Learning Difficulties (SLD)
P6		
P7		
P8		
1		
2	Average 7-year-old	Pupils working within this range of levels are usually described as having Moderate Learning Difficulties (MLD)
3		
4	Average 11-year-old	
5	Average 14-year-old	
6		
7		
8	A good GCSE result	

Breaking down learning into small steps over a series of lessons

It is important you are able to break key skills down for your pupils. Discussions with your class teacher and use of assessment schemes will help you prepare for this. By examining planning from the previous half term you will be able to see how the needs of the pupils and progression are planned for. The challenge for any teacher is how to encourage and motivate a pupil to meet their potential whilst at the same time not overwhelming them.

 Key questions to consider

- What do you want the pupils to learn during the session you are planning?
- What are the skills they will need to be able to achieve that outcome?
- How will you identify the steps pupils will need to go through to succeed?
- How do you plan to overcome their barriers to learning?

You will need to be able to identify the next steps in the learning process so that you can give feedback to the pupil and plan further learning opportunities. You will also need to know when a pupil needs additional practice to consolidate their knowledge and understanding. This is achieved through the process of 'assess, plan, do and review'.

Using reflective lesson evaluations to inform future planning

Critical reflection/evaluation/review of each of your lessons are crucial to inform your future planning and need to be based on evidence from observations, pupil responses/engagement, notes and other evidence in terms of pupils' progress (in the form of photographs, video or pupils' work). You are required to use your best endeavours to make sure that pupils get the support they need, achieve their best and become confident individuals (DfE, 2014b). You need to be mindful of this when reviewing the successes and areas to develop in terms of your teaching and use the information to inform your future planning.

Points to consider when critically reflecting on a lesson

- What went well, with evidence of how you know?
- Which pedagogical choices were most effective and why?
- What did each pupil respond to in a positive way?
- What did not go well and why not?
- Were the pupils engaged, and how do you know?
- Was there an impact on learning, what evidence do you have?
- Were resources suitable and at the right level for the class?
- Were the adults effectively deployed during the session, and how did they further the learning?
- Did the pupils let you know how well they thought they did?
- What might have worked better?
- Were there any misconceptions you need to address?
- What will you change next time, and how will you and the team plan for this?

It is important that the outcome of your reflections is evident in future planning. For example, if you identify that a pupil was unable to access the activity due to distractions from another pupil, you need highlight on your next daily lesson plan that these two pupils must be kept apart. Teaching is an accountable profession, therefore you must ensure that you maintain thorough and detailed records of pupil progress.

Preparing pupils for transition readiness

Pupils must be well prepared for any changes that are going to take place in their school life; this includes moving from one class to another, one Key Stage to another and into adulthood. It also includes transitions within and around the school. Many pupils in specialist provision find change very difficult, so it is important to keep to a routine as far as possible. It may be that certain groups of pupils have a slightly different routine to others to reduce anxiety. An example of this would be not moving pupils with autism around the school when large groups are changing lesson.

Larger and more significant transitions such as class and Key Stage changes can pose an immense challenge for the individual involved, particularly when they encounter barriers in communication and interaction. It is common for schools to give a member of staff a specific role in managing transitions from one provision to another or one school to another.

Other barriers to learning to consider

- Over stimulation through the environment or the proximity of other pupils in the room.
- Certain noises that are sometimes imperceptible to others can cause distress, anxiety and even anger.
- Lack of teacher knowledge to facilitate effective communication.
- Sensory impairments such as hearing or visual impairment, or in a more extreme case tactile defensive individuals – this is where an individual has an aversion to exploring a range of objects and materials of different form and texture.
- Difficulties with attention, such as high levels of distractibility and low concentration levels.
- Medical issues, which can cause fatigue.
- Physical difficulties, which may have an impact on access.
- Psychological issues, including mental health issues.

(Continued)

(Continued)

- Processing difficulties, so teachers must ensure that individuals have enough time to process and respond to questions and instructions.
- Ineffective deployment of staff, resulting in poor pupil outcomes.
- Lack of appropriate and engaging resources.
- Hunger, lack of nourishment and dehydration, and the inability to articulate these needs.
- Lack of sleep.

One of the greatest challenges trainee teachers encounter is knowing how to begin planning for the first time. You need to prepare by meeting with the class teacher and the planning team to develop an understanding of how the planning is approached, which frameworks are used and the current attainment and specific needs of the pupils. Without this information you will not be able to begin planning. It is also important that you are aware of the pupil's individual interests and what they respond well to in terms of teaching approaches. In a specialist context the planning will require you to have a detailed knowledge of each pupil you are teaching. You will need to understand their particular needs in terms of triggers for behaviours and anxieties, what motivates them to learn and participate and what their individual targets are. In terms of their targets, the EHC plan will include targets spanning from current date to adulthood. To plan effectively you must also know their learning preferences. How do the pupils in your class prefer to work – alone, in a group, with/ without music, using technology, practical activities or by moving around (physical)? If you know their preferences you can accommodate these into your planning, when appropriate.

 Key points to remember

- Use alternatives to written recording and outline these in your planning: photographs, art work, drama, drawing, video capture or using outdoor materials to inspire and develop skills in writing and recording.
- Some pupils will need a variety of short activities followed by an activity of their choice.

- Find strategies that work for the individual pupil that allow them to access learning and overcome their barriers; for example, some pupils may benefit from a three-point approach (First … then … after).
- Use effective reward systems that you have seen in use in your own schools, such as a behaviour chart with negotiated and desirable rewards.
- Use positive language, such as 'walking sensibly' rather than 'don't run', 'good sitting' rather than 'sit up straight'.
- Incorporate individual pupils' interests into planning.
- Extended periods of sitting and waiting can cause anxiety and distress for some individuals.
- Identify a quiet area ready for pupils who get distressed.
- Use a system such as traffic light cards or smiley faces to communicate if they can't cope or require time out.

Planning in the EYFS is very different to planning for Key Stages 1, 2, 3, 4 and post 16. For the Key Stages 1–4 and post 16 you will have programmes of work, whether thematic or subject based. The EYFS for children 0–5 years is a play-based framework which is planned purposeful play, with both child- and adult-led activities. Every EYFS context will be planned in a unique way, so it is impossible to give a set planning format to use (please see the online extras for exemplar proformas).

The EYFS (DfE, 2014b) comprises three prime and four specific areas of learning and development. The prime areas are evident in daily practice and are described as the foundations of learning. They are: Communication and Language; Physical Development; and Personal, Social and Emotional Development. The specific areas are: Literacy; Mathematics; Understanding the World; and Expressive Arts and Design.

These seven areas are all interlinked and must be evident in your planning. As pupils enter the nursery through to the end of reception at five years the planning should be based upon the interests, needs and stages of development of the children. In light of this it is futile to plan for six weeks of learning on transport, for example. You may find their interest in transport lasts only for three days and you would then need to re-plan for the other weeks. Because of this it is advisable to plan for a few days at a time so you can be responsive to the pupils' interests, wishes and needs.

In Key Stages 1, 2, 3, 4 and post 16, the planning structures will be easier to follow. The medium-term planning will usually be broken down into six-week 'chunks'. It may be subject or theme based, and it will be flexible in terms of how you derive your individual lessons from it. As with all planning you need to be organised; ensure that you find out what you need to know to be able to plan effectively prior to your time in school commencing. In all specialist contexts there is a focus on planning for outdoor learning, trips, visits to local amenities and incorporating the local environment. If you are taking the pupils out of the school environment it is imperative that you complete a risk assessment.

 Key points to remember

- Meet with the planning team in advance of your placement commencing so that you know what you will be expected to teach in terms of the theme, subject or pupils' interests.
- Spend time in school getting to know the pupils you will be teaching before your teaching begins.
- Ask the school for copies of medium-term plans that currently exist, as you can use these as a start point.
- Ask the school which planning proformas you should use. If you are in teacher training your provider may request you to plan in a certain way. You need to be flexible, as the school may request that you plan in a different way.
- If you are in an early years context it is unlikely that there will be medium-term plans, as most contexts have detailed daily plans instead. Each pupil will have a key person who you need to liaise with in terms of their individual needs and interests.
- Seek advice and guidance on completing a risk assessment if you are taking the pupils off site.
- Find out the pupils' current levels of attainment and progression targets.
- Find out how and when you will engage with parents and carers.
- Find out how to track progress for the whole class and individual pupils.

 Reflective activity

You are working in a Year 5 class of seven pupils who all have SLD. Each morning two pupils need to be taken from their wheelchairs and placed on the floor to have their arms and legs stretched, and then to be placed over a wedge for 30 minutes. This is part of their learning plan and they have targets that have to be met.

The targets of the two pupils are:

Mathematics: Shape, Space and Measure (P7) 'To respond to forwards and backwards, moving forwards and backwards on request'.

Literacy: Speaking and Listening (P6) 'To take turns in a paired game' and 'To follow instructions with three key words'.

The first lesson each morning is Mathematics. What kind of activities would you prepare for the two pupils, incorporating their targets, and how would you deploy your support staff? (Some suggestions are given at the end of the chapter.)

Additional resources

As well as the resources you'll find at **www.sagepub.co.uk/martindenham** you should also take a look at the following:

Department for Education (DfE) (2010) *Progression 2010–2011: Advice on Improving Data to Raise Attainment and Maximise the Progress of Learners with Special Educational Needs.* London: DfE

Department for Education (DfE) (2013a) *National Curriculum in England: Primary Curriculum.* Available at www.gov.uk/government/publications/national-curriculum-in-england-primary-curriculum. This link includes the programmes of study and attainment targets for Key Stages 1 and 2.

Department for Education (DfE) (2013b) *National Curriculum in England: Secondary Curriculum.* Available at www.gov.uk/government/publications/national-curriculum-in-england-secondary-curriculum. This link includes the programmes of study and attainment targets for Key Stages 3 and 4.

Department for Education (DfE) (2014a) *Special Educational Needs and Disability Code of Practice: 0–25 Years.* Statutory guidance for organisations who work with and support young people with SEND. London. DfE. This is essential reading in preparation for teaching pupil, pages 86–87 provide clarity on the broad areas of need.

Department for Education (DfE) (2014b) *Statutory Framework for the Early Years Foundation Stage.* London: DfE. This is the framework for the EYFS and is essential reading if you are in an early years context. You also must have a copy of *Development Matters* (Early Education, 2012), which is supported by the DfE as it is the non-statutory guidance materials which are essential for planning towards the Early Learning Goals. This can be found at www.early-education.org.uk/development-matters (accessed August 2014).

(Continued)

(Continued)

Department for Education (DfE) (2014c) *Performance-P Scale-Attainment Targets for Pupils with Special Educational Needs*. London:DfE.

The Dyslexia-Specific Learning Disability (SpLD) Trust provide a very useful website: www.interventionsforliteracy.org.uk. The website includes an extensive list of rated interventions that you can use with pupils across the age phases.

Using the P Scales, www.nasen.org.uk/pscales/. This is a useful area of the website to explore as it includes PowerPoint slides from training sessions held by NASEN (National Association for Special Educational Needs) on the curriculum, using the P scales, and what is good progress for pupils with SEN.

Possible solutions

For the Reflective activity on p. 46

If pupils are age 11 and working at P7 they are unlikely to make three levels of progress BUT individual challenge could be planned by:

- specific individual targets carefully tailored to the individual pupil based on a thorough knowledge of their strengths, needs and abilities;
- activities that enthuse the pupil based on their particular interests;
- ownership of their learning so that they understand where they are starting and what they are aiming for (in simple terms and short steps);
- achievable challenges set so that progress can be seen beginning with very easy challenges building in difficulty;
- achievement shown visually on the classroom wall so they can see that they are making progress.

For the Reflective activity on p. 52–53

The TA could be employed to work with the two pupils with a bullet-pointed instruction sheet. Pupils should be placed facing each other so that they can have eye contact and the maximum opportunity to interact and take turns. They could have a laminated grid on the floor and be asked to move two cars 'forwards 3 squares' or 'backwards 1 square': this would complete their Literacy target. Each pupil could comment on whether the other had been successful. The activity could also be achieved using Bee-Bots® (programmable floor robot). The session could start with the both pupils being encouraged to move their arms forwards and backwards so that these concepts could be checked.

CHAPTER 6

ASSESSING LEARNING

Judith Donovan, Dawn Henderson,
Pauline James and Sarah Martin-Denham

Key ideas explored in this chapter

- How to assess progress
- Formative assessment and tracking pupil progress
- Questioning as an assessment tool
- Assessing learning
- Gaining feedback from pupils with profound and multiple learning difficulties (PMLD)
- Assessment for Learning (AFL)
- Summative assessment
- How to use national and school-based data

This chapter builds on Chapter 4, Teaching and Learning and Chapter 5, Planning for Learning.

How to assess progress

As in a mainstream context, those in specialist provision need to have their progress assessed to ensure the setting is having an impact on their learning and development. Within the role as teacher you will continually review the progress your pupils are making in all lessons through observation, marking, feedback and discussion with the team. You will need to decide how you will track and review the progress of the pupils you are teaching so that any adaptations to the teaching, provision, resources and learning environment can be made promptly. The purpose of assessment is to place the pupil at a certain level and to use this knowledge to help them to progress to the next stage. Assessment is also the means by which you begin to plan for pupil progression within individual lessons and over periods of time. As a teacher you can use assessment outcomes to provide a rationale as to how you are building on prior achievement and to reflect on your own practice. Effective learning occurs when the teacher has accurately assessed the pupil and then plans high-quality, creative lessons based upon high expectations and the pupils' interests.

In a specialist setting, the issue is how to assess accurately pupils who often make such small steps of progress. They cannot be assessed using the same systems as those pupils who make age-expected progress, and as a result staff need to consider a range of ways of monitoring and assessing the progress of the whole child. As part of your role in school you will need to use a range of assessment strategies within your day-to-day practice to monitor progress and to inform your future planning. The challenge is to be able to assess pupil progress through a range of methods; remember that many pupils will not be able to record their work in the usual way (completing worksheets, writing down their thoughts and expressing themselves).

Many pupils will not be able to tell you how well they have understood something as their method of communication may not be through speech (they may use signing, gesture, symbols, movement or facial expressions) or they may need your well developed questioning skills to help them to realise what they do know. The teacher needs to be familiar with which method a pupil is able to use and facilitate their communication in an attempt to understand how they have progressed.

Some pupils will need an advocate to be their voice. In a specialist setting this will often be a key person/worker/staff member who works closely with that pupil and with whom they have formed a strong bond. Working closely with parents and carers is also crucial, as they know their child and will often be able to advise staff about how they are likely to react in a variety of situations.

There may be times when you have planned to carry out an assessment but the pupil may not be compliant; in these situations you may need to re-schedule to a different time or day. It may be through assessments that you identify that a pupil is not making progress or is unable to access the curriculum. You will need to discuss this with the SENCO and class teacher to ensure that barriers to learning are identified and where possible overcome. You cannot make judgements on a pupil's level of working based upon one assessment, you will need to gain evidence from a range of methods of assessment over a period of time.

Formative assessment tracks pupil progress throughout the teaching process whilst summative assessment highlights progress over given periods of time (usually a school year). It is important to be aware of how systematic assessment is carried out in the school in which you are working as many variations are used. The school will also have an 'assessment policy' which will tell you key information that you will need to be familiar with.

Formative assessment and tracking pupil progress

Formative assessment is your systematic, ongoing day-to-day process used to monitor pupils' knowledge and understanding and to improve and modify your own practice. Throughout each lesson you will need to check and note understanding to ensure that you are having a positive impact on the learning. This involves verifying the progress pupils are making and identifying appropriate interventions/learning opportunities/targets to support further progress. Schools will have their favoured system to collect information about progress in relation to the tracking systems they are using, such as PIVATS or B Squared. The methods of recording what you are assessing can include narrative accounts from participant and non-participant observations, notes from questions asked, work samples, concept mapping, digital recordings of peer groups and self-assessment.

You will need to track and analyse the data you collect to inform your future teaching. Often the data will tell a story, too: if pupils have medical issues, have family difficulties or missed school for other reasons, there may be indicators of regression. As professionals you will need to know the full story before making conclusions about progress or lack of it. Tracking and interrogating data is very important to ensure that issues and trends are identified and interventions put into place. As the teacher you will be accountable for the progress each pupil is making.

Within every system, each pupil, group of pupils, and subject area will have been analysed and data will be available to inform your teaching. Be aware that data should be available for pupils in various vulnerability groups, such as those with SEN, looked after/adopted children, pupils with disabilities and those who receive free school meals (FSM), also known as 'unseen children'. Unseen children are described as those from disadvantaged families who experience social and economic disadvantage. In 2012 the Department for Education reported that only 38 per cent of pupils eligible for FSM gained five or more GCSEs including Mathematics and English in comparison to 66 per cent of all other pupils (DfE, 2012a). It is because of this that in 2014 schools were again provided with additional funding for each pupil who is entitled to FSM to use towards improving their outcomes.

Assessment over time, including judgements made while marking class work and homework, observations, pupil voice, pupil questions and their feedback, all combine to give a rounded picture of the pupil and how they learn. This is then all combined to decide on the levels they are considered to have reached, and this begins the circle of teaching, learning, assessment and evaluation. Schools may use methods of triangulating evidence to ensure that they have a full picture of the pupils' learning. This is also used as evidence of monitoring towards Ofsted inspections (see Table 6.1).

As part of the assessment process you need to be mindful of how you will include the pupils in the self-assessment process. You must provide regular feedback on the learning that is taking place, and ensure that pupils have opportunities to share what they have learned and understand what they need to do next to improve. In a specialist context you need to consider the most appropriate way to do this. Using clear and concise language once you have the attention of the pupil is a good starting point.

 Reflective activity

A pupil has been practising letter formation of the letter 'S' with the teacher. The pupil has progressed from forming the letter 'S' in the sand and gloop and has just formed the letter correctly for the first time on paper.

This is the conversation between the teacher and the pupil:

Pupil: 'I have finished.'
Teacher: 'That is good, well done.'

What is missing from the feedback process? Has the teacher identified 'what was good'? Has the pupil been encouraged to talk about their achievement? Re-write the conversation considering effective feedback strategies which include opportunities for celebration, reflection and future aspirations.

Table 6.1 Triangulation of evidence

Teacher:

Ofsted Criteria:	Observation evidence	Work scrutiny evidence	Pupils' voice evidence (where possible)	Progress evidence
Work is challenging enough for all pupils and meets their individual needs.				
Pupils' responses demonstrate sufficient gains in their knowledge, skills and understanding, including in literacy and maths.				
Teachers monitor pupils' progress in lessons and use their information well to adapt their teaching.				
Teachers and support staff use questioning to assess the effectiveness of their teaching and promote pupils' learning.				
Pupils understand how to improve their work.				
Pupils' engagement, interest, concentration, determination, resilience and independence (where possible).				
Core skills in teaching; planning, implementing learning activities, marking, assessment and feedback, and setting appropriate homework (where appropriate). High levels of expertise and subject knowledge.				

It is likely that the school in which you work will have a form of whole-school monitoring to identify those pupils who are not making expected levels of progress despite quality first teaching. This could be on an individual, class or whole school basis, or could be looking deeper into the progress of particular groups such as those on FSM, looked after children, those with disabilities or pupil premium in relation to NC levels/P scales/PIVATS. The evidence of progress can be derived from sources such as observations by the senior management team, work scrutiny, assessed work, moderation events and use of assessing pupil progress (APP). As part of the progress, meeting strategies will be put into place to ensure that targets relating to the expectations of progress are met. As a teacher it is essential that you have a full overview of the holistic development of the pupil and up-to-date projected targets for the year. It would also be useful to know the targets for the previous year so that you are aware of usual rates of progress for individual pupils.

 **Key questions to consider**

- Do I have a full picture of the pupils' prior and current attainment in all areas of learning, such as personal and social skills, barriers to learning as well as academic levels?
- Have I used the pupils' current attainment levels as a start point for my planning?
- Can I assess pupils' learning through questioning techniques?
- How will I ensure that I progress learning with an appropriate level of challenge?
- What will I need to do to track pupils' ongoing progress during my time in school, do I know the school systems for this?
- How can I demonstrate a high level of responsibility for the attainment, progress and outcomes of the individual pupils I teach?
- How can I involve the pupils in setting future targets based upon their achievements?

 Reflective activity

Up-to-date information is not available on the pupils' current level of working, due to a change in staffing. Who could support you in ensuring that your planning is set at the appropriate level for the pupils? (Some suggestions are given at the end of the chapter.)

Questioning as an assessment tool

Throughout each lesson you will need to ensure that you use a range of open and closed questions to determine the level of understanding in relation to the learning objectives. In a special-ist context the use of open and closed questions is an essential way of making judgements on how effective your lesson is at furthering and consolidating learning. As a method of assess-ment, questioning is an essential tool and needs to be incorpo-rated in each lesson plan. You may wish to consider targeting questions to certain pupils at key points during the lesson. The use of mini-plenaries is a highly effective way of assessing the pupil's understanding of your intentions at different points during a lesson. They are also useful in reminding pupils who may have working memory difficulties what they are doing and why throughout the lesson.

Assessing learning

Assessing learning is an ongoing process which informs planning on a day-to-day, if not lesson-to-lesson, basis. Good feedback systems need to be in place so that the teacher has as much information as possible about the progress of pupils, so that judgements can be made as to whether a pupil has understood/mastered a concept, needs further practice, needs further modelling or needs to be moved on. A rigorous feedback system needs to be set up between the teacher and support staff, and the teacher/support staff and the pupil.

 Reflective activity

Can you list the ways a teacher can ensure that the assessment carried out in their classroom supports them in planning lessons to ensure that their pupils make as much progress as possible? Consider the following:

- How staff give feedback to pupils.
- How pupils can assess their own learning.
- How pupils can support each others' learning.
- How staff can share feedback.
- How teachers ensure that assessment judgements are accurate.

Gaining feedback from pupils with profound and multiple learning difficulties (PMLD)

When providing for pupils with complex needs it can be difficult for them to express their views, so systems need to be in place to ensure that pupils are enabled to give an opinion on their own progress. You need to be clear that pupils have understood their goals and that they understand how they will be assessed. Learning objectives must be accessible to the pupils, yourself and the other adults working in the class. It is vital that pupils are aware of what they, or other pupils, need to do to progress, and that they are able to give this information to staff in whichever way they can. Some pupils may need an advocate to feedback for them, usually someone who knows the pupil and can identify signs of understanding and enjoyment. Some pupils' main method of communication may be to smile, move an arm or leg, eye point or use facial expressions. A member of staff finely tuned to this pupil needs to be on hand to feedback their wants and desires and progress.

In some settings a 'progress wall' is used to share and view learning objectives and for pupils to view, assess and track their own progress. These walls are often used before and after lessons for pupils with severe and complex learning disabilities. They are usually symbol based and are able to be used in an interactive way between the pupil and the adults in the class.

Celebrating success makes the assessment circle complete. Pupils must be rewarded, in order for further learning to be a positive experience, and there is no greater reward than the positive regard shown by peers and staff, in whom the pupil has invested their vulnerability, trust and confidence.

Here are some examples of how pupils can be supported to share their knowledge and understanding:

- *Traffic lights*: red, amber and green in the form of hand-held cards.
- *Smiley faces*: displaying emotions, happy, sad, frustrated.
- *Targets boards/progress wall*: to support peer- and self-assessment through signs and symbols to indicate progress that has been made in an individual lesson.
- *Pupil evaluation cards*: using Communicate: In Print picture symbols.

Using challenge to motivate pupils

Two 15-year-old pupils, David and Scott, in provision for pupils with autism were engaging in a mathematics activity to read bus and train timetables. They were asked a number of questions, individually, about which bus they would need to get to catch a train to go to a variety of destinations. While David was answering his question, the teacher noticed that Scott was not engaged. He had been asked to work out the answer, silently, himself but he obviously needed some structure in place to keep him on task. So the teacher gave him a small whiteboard on which to write the answer, and a clock with moving hands, so that he could calculate it. Scott was set the task of finding the answer before David. He found this very motivating, found the correct answer very quickly, and could be heard to encourage David 'Come on David, hurry up'. Once it was David's turn he responded in the same way, and both pupils were able to find the answer to the question much more quickly when it was their friend's turn.

Assessment for Learning (AfL)

Assessment for Learning (AfL) is a type of formative assessment used in many schools. The Assessment for Learning Strategy was launched in 2008 by the Department for Children, Schools and Families with the purpose of encouraging schools in the process of seeking and interpreting evidence for use by learners and their teachers to decide where the learners are in their learning, where they need to go and how best to get there (DCSF, 2008).

Schools may use AfL as an integral part of their planning, to focus on how pupils learn, to establish the level of achievement, where they might go next and how best to get there. AfL is based on the principle that pupils will improve most if they understand the aim of the learning, where they are in relation to it and how they can achieve it. It encourages the pupil to take responsibility for their own learning, and that of others, and helps them to know how to improve, and it enables parents and carers to know how their child is progressing, what they need to do to improve and how they can support their child.

As part of this initiative the then Government also introduced APP (Assessing Pupil Progress), which was a structured approach to tracking pupil progress. The APP guidance provides an approach to making judgements on levels and sublevels across Key Stages and subjects.

 Key points to remember

- Consider how the class teacher you are working with uses AfL on a day-to-day basis.
- Examine how each pupil in your class communicates their understanding of how well they are doing.
- Share learning objectives with the pupils and negotiate the success criteria.
- Identify systems you will use to ensure that at the end of each teaching session you are clear about what the pupils have learned.
- Make sure the other adults working in your class are able to feedback to you how well the pupil/s they have been working with have managed the activity.
- Ensure that support staff give you information specifically around the learning outcome (and success criteria) for that session.
- Although it is important that pupils are encouraged and praised, they also need to know what they did well and what they need to do next. Adults must find ways to communicate this to the pupils as well as be able to give you that information to inform your future planning.
- Get to know how the pupils in your class communicate so that you are able to identify how much they have understood.

Summative assessment

This is an assessment which is carried out after a period of time, usually at the end of the school year, although some schools will carry out end-of-term assessments or half-yearly assessments. Summative assessments are used to inform national data such as P scales, NC tests and examinations. In specialist contexts the number of pupils who take end of Key Stage Standard Assessment Tests (SATs) including the Year 1 Phonics Screen will vary. There are certain exemptions in national tests for pupils with SEN. For example, pupils who show no understanding of grapheme-phoneme awareness, those newly arrived to the country, mute or selectively mute, or some who use British Sign Language, would not be entered for the Year 1 phonics screening check. For some types of provision there won't be any pupils entered for the end of Key Stage Tests (SATs) due to their particular needs. Assessment of pupil progress is undertaken by the teacher, but with as much information as possible from all adults working with the pupil, and the pupil themselves. Teacher judgements must be moderated as there are usually strong elements of subjectivity, and disagreements can arise between practitioners about levels. Statements of assessment can sometimes be ambiguous, so it is important that a well understood baseline level is set so that all involved have the same understanding of what is expected at a particular level. Good practice within special educational provision is for staff to have moderation opportunities, both within the setting where they work and, when possible, sharing with other similar settings.

Data analysis systems are used to show where pupils are succeeding and where they are facing difficulties. Teachers should be using data to support their planning. Systems such as Comparison and Analysis of Special Pupil Attainment (CASPA) and the Durham P Scales Project use national data to produce information showing how pupils are achieving, in comparison to pupils with similar needs. This information can help support judgements of how well pupils are achieving. The P scales are generally used for pupils whose progress falls outside of national expectations. The PIVATS assessment system breaks down the P scales into five smaller steps to allow more accurate assessment (further information on PIVATS can be found in Chapter 5).

Other assessment systems used include:

- Developmental check between the ages of two and two and a half years by a Health Visitor.
- Early Years Foundation Stage Profile (EYFS).
- Year 1 Statutory Phonics Screen.
- B Squared.
- PIVATS.
- Standard Assessment Tests (SATs).

Once it is established at which level a pupil is working and how best to facilitate learning for that pupil, then the curriculum content of the NC, or other curricula such as the Primary International Curriculum, can be interpreted to suit the pupil's needs. It should never be that the pupil is made to 'fit' the curriculum. Equally, there are a variety of awarding bodies such as ASDAN (Award Scheme Development and Accreditation Network), NOCN (National Open College Network) and OCR (Oxford, Cambridge and RSA) that provide awards and qualifications for post 16 pupils directly correlated to their level of attainment, so it is vital that their current working level is established accurately.

 Reflective activity

Which of the annotations below gives the pupil the most support in order to progress in their learning, and why? Which gives the teacher more information to plan for the next session, and why?

1. *Learning objective*: To distinguish between 'more than' → and 'less than' ←

'Good work! You have written the number 5 really neatly.'

2. *Learning objective*: To identify pictures with beginning with the sound 'e'

'You found the pictures that started with the sound 'e' although you were a little unsure about the pictures you left, but you soon worked out they weren't the correct sound. You can try a few more next time! Well done!'

How to use national and school-based data

As part of your role as a trainee teacher you need to be able to confidently and accurately assess pupils' attainment against national benchmarks. In order to do this you need to have a secure understanding of statutory assessment requirements for the subjects/curriculum/frameworks you are teaching.

It is important to understand that data only becomes effective if it promotes critical reflection and questioning about the actual learning that is taking place and considers how learning can be developed further. A vital part in the effective use of data is the inclusion of meaningful dialogue between staff, departments and faculties to ensure that the data remains a reflective and relevant tool to plan forward from.

Data is essential to the Ofsted inspection framework and is used to evaluate school performance and progress. Ofsted inspections will focus on the achievement of pupils at the school, including groups of pupils discussed earlier in the chapter (Ofsted, 2014). Schools need to demonstrate how they are using their data to analyse progress and to target-set for the future. RAISEonline is a system which some schools are using to analyse their data in depth as part of their self-evaluation process. In your school there is likely to be a key person who has a role and responsibility for using data to move learning forward, either by focussing on specific areas or supporting colleagues in the interpretation of outcomes. In some schools this support is given in the form of a termly learning conversation or data progress meeting.

Finding the space and time to input, update and analyse data is the main challenge to the effective use of data. It is important that, in terms of data, you become familiar with the systems in place in your school, follow the tracking process through and if in doubt ask questions to gain clarification. Data is a positive intervention to ensure that the pupils in our care progress to the best of their ability. It should not be viewed singly as a monitoring tool for teaching and learning.

 Reflective activity

It has been highlighted in the termly data progress meeting that the trail of data that you have about a particular pupil in your class does not reflect the expectation of their progress.

What other information would you bring to the meeting as evidence that this may not be entirely related to school learning? How would you present a plan for this pupil to ensure that progress is secure? (Some suggestions are given at the end of the chapter.)

Additional resources

As well as the resources you'll find at **www.sagepub.co.uk/martindenham** you should also take a look at the following:

B Squared, www.bsquared.co.uk/: By clicking on the 'Assessment files' link on the navigation bar you can find out further information about the B Squared small steps assessment scheme, which can be used from the EYFS to post 16.

Centre for Evaluation and Monitoring (CEM), www.cem.org/pscales: The aim of this website is to improve teaching and learning for all children and young people. It provides research-based tracking systems for monitoring pupils' progress.

Department of Children, Schools and Families (2008) *The Assessment for Learning Strategy.* Nottingham: DCSF. This guide will provide you with information on how to use AfL to enhance learning and improve the rates at which pupils progress.

(Continued)

(Continued)

Office for Standards in Education (Ofsted) (2013) *Unseen Children: Access and Achievement 20 Years On: Evidence Report.* London: Ofsted. A useful report to develop your knowledge and understanding as to why some children who live with social and economic disadvantage have lower educational outcomes.

Office for Standards in Education (Ofsted) (2014) *The Framework for School Inspection.* London: Ofsted. This is the current Ofsted inspection framework that you need to be familiar with regardless of the educational context you are in.

PIVATS, www.lancashire.gov.uk/corporate/web/?PIVATS/14585: This website will provide you with guidance and information on using PIVATS from NC level 1 to NC level 4 for assessment, target setting and monitoring.

Times Education Supplement (TES), www.tes.co.uk/TaxonomySearchResults.aspx?keywords=assessment&parametrics=52004: This web link takes you to the SEN section and includes lots of APP/PIVATS tracking grids, target sheets, self-assessment proformas for assessing and monitoring pupil progress.

Possible solutions

For the Reflective activity on p. 60

- Arrange to meet with the SENCO, who will be able to tell you the most recent levels of working from school monitoring systems.
- Examine previous planning, which will give you a sense of where the pupils were working and the progress they made.
- Speak to the support staff who are/were working with the pupils you are teaching, as they should be able to provide you with valuable information.

For the Reflective activity on p. 67

In this situation you need to present the data you have on the pupil, which will show their start point at the beginning of your placement and the progress they have made since that point. You may also have other information regarding the pupil which is not in the actual data. This may include a period of absence, change or adjustment in medication or a change in family circumstances which would explain the pupil not achieving the expectations. If you keep up-to-date records, tracking progress and evaluating to inform future teaching, you will be able to discuss with confidence the next steps of learning and development for the pupil. Also, the mentor overseeing your placement will be able to support you in meetings as they will have retained some teaching responsibility for the class and will be able to endorse your evidence.

CHAPTER 7

WORKING IN PARTNERSHIP WITH FAMILIES, PARENTS AND CARERS

Denise Murray

Key ideas explored in this chapter

- Different types of families
- Why work in collaboration with parents and carers?
- Communication by email/text message
- What to do when you need to report an incident with another pupil

---

This chapter will focus on developing your skills and confidence in working in collaboration with parents and carers. One of the underlying principles of the *Special Educational Needs and Disability Code of Practice* (DfE, 2014a) is that the views, wishes and feelings of the child or young person, and the child's parents, must be taken into account by the LA. This is to ensure that the child and the parents are involved in the discussions and decisions about their individual support. The intention is that parents or the young person are fully included and meaningfully engaged in the assessment for the EHC plan and that they are consulted throughout the process. Quite often parents of children with SEND have had to fight to get the education they feel is right for their child. In light of this, some may approach each situation as a battle. As practitioners in schools we need to show parents that this is not the case and we want to work with them for the best outcomes for their child.

Different types of families

One danger we must not fall into is prejudging parents. Not everyone lives the same way as we do, or holds the same values; that does not make them wrong, just different from our families. As professionals we have to be non-judgemental in every interaction we have with parents.

There are many different types of families, which may be similar to or different from your own. It is essential that in your teaching you acknowledge the diversity of the range of families that exist. Some children will live with a mother and a father or with one parent. Others may live with two mothers or two fathers, grandparents or be in the care system or adopted. All schools have a legal obligation to recognise difference through the Equality Act 2010.

 Reflective activity

Daisy, age seven, lives with her two mothers from Monday to Friday. On a Friday evening she is collected from school by her father and his female partner who she stays with until the Sunday evening. The family often meet up for meals and take Daisy out as one family. The mothers, father and step-mother all like to remain informed of Daisy's progress in school. How would you ensure that all of Daisy's family are kept up to date about her achievements and progress in school?

Why work in collaboration with parents/carers?

Working with parents can be one of the most rewarding aspects of being a teacher; however, it can also be one of the most challenging parts of the profession. It is essential to remember that everyone wants the same thing, what they believe is the best for the child.

It is imperative that you introduce yourself to the parents as soon as you can, be it at the beginning of the school year, placement or as soon as a new child joins your group. You will be spending at least five hours a day with their most precious possession. Parents need to know that their child is in safe hands and have confidence and faith in the team who are teaching and supporting them. The first impressions can determine what kind of relationship you will have with the parents.

Informal but professional communication is often the best way to form a working relationship. When introducing yourself to parents use your full name; that way parents can choose how to address you. In future communications you may choose to use your first name, for example, 'Hello, it's Denise from Barbara Priestman School'. This way parents/carers will feel they can address you in whatever way they find most comfortable.

In special educational provision you need to build a working relationship with all parents and carers, particularly those who rarely come into school. Lack of communication is a frequent cause for complaint on Ofsted parental questionnaires, with parents feeling that school is uninterested in their views. Most schools only ring parents regarding negative incidents and this can have a detrimental effect on the parent–teacher relationship. Nothing is more pleasing than when I ring a new parent for the first time and they say 'Oh no what have they done now?' and I can respond by saying 'Well, you are not going to believe this but they have been excellent in maths today, they found it difficult but they didn't give up and tried their best.' Sharing good news means that when you do need to speak to parents about negative behaviour it is not the norm, so parents take it seriously and are not on the defensive.

 Key points to remember

- If the school uses a home/school planner write in it regularly, because this can be the only daily means of communication as often children are not particularly eager to tell parents about their day.
- It is important to make parents/carers feel comfortable when communicating with them, therefore when talking to parents be a chameleon and adapt the way you speak to fit in with them. Think about the vocabulary and the terminology used.
- If you receive a phone call, return it as soon as possible, otherwise ask someone else to ring on your behalf and say when you will be in touch. This immediate acknowledgement signals to parents that the message has been passed on and gives them an idea of when they can expect a response.

If a telephone call does not resolve an issue, you need to have a face-to-face meeting. While making the appointment say how long you have available, for example 'I can meet you at 9 o'clock Monday morning but I am teaching at 10'. That way everyone knows the timescale from the outset and another date and time can be booked if necessary.

CASE STUDY

Acronyms

While working in an all-age special school I attended a meeting with parents and professionals during which many acronyms were used, such as SLD, ADHD and ASAP. At the end of the meeting the parents took me to one side and asked if their child had ASAP. At first I was confused and asked 'Where did you hear that?' and they recounted the conversation, so I immediately explained what ASAP stands for. This shows how easy it is to confuse parents, so avoid using jargon and check that they understand what has been said.

Communication by email/text message

Communication can take different forms. The majority of parents like to communicate by email as they can email or respond at a convenient time. If the parent is in a heightened state of anxiety, it is likely an email is not appropriate so arrange a face-to-face meeting for as soon as is convenient for both parties. Consider the following key points when you are emailing a parent.

 Key points to remember

- Check the school is happy for you to email parents; a member of the senior management team may wish to view it before it is sent.
- Use a school email address not a personal one.
- Consider whether an email is the best way to communicate with the parent on certain matters.
- If you are annoyed or upset do not email a parent, as emails cannot be retracted.
- Keep all emails professional; never write anything in an email you would not want other people to read.

A relatively new form of communication is 'Text 2 Parents', a text service which allows schools to text every parent with the same message: this could be to a Key Stage, particular year group or individual parents. This is popular as most parents own a mobile telephone. As with emails, all texts to parents should not contain 'text speak' as they are professional communications. It is important to remember that not every parent has the literacy skills to read a letter, email or text, and it is imperative that you discover this as early as possible so that alternative means of communication can be found.

 Reflective activity

A parent has not been attending school events and has failed to return a consent form for a school trip which you are organising. The school suspects that the parent has difficulties with reading.

    What would you do in this situation? (Some suggestions are given at the end of the chapter.)

What to do when you need to report an incident with another pupil

Honesty is the best policy when working with parents. However, when telling parents about an incident involving their child and another pupil, you must never disclose the other pupil's name. Their child will probably say who it was. Explain to the parent that you are not able to discuss other pupils with them, just as you wouldn't if their child had been involved in an incident. Parents appreciate this as they would not want their child being discussed without their knowledge.

 Key points to remember

- Ensure that you know all the facts about an incident before speaking to parents.
- Check that the school's behaviour policy has been followed in relation to sanctions.
- Ensure that all pupils are treated equally and fairly.

As practitioners we only see the child in the school context and they can behave very differently at home to the way they present in school. Listen to the concerns of parents and, more importantly, hear what they are saying. Parents have known their children longer than you have. A useful way to do this is to say 'I am listening to what you have to say and I heard ...' (repeat back to them what they have said). By doing this you are showing they have your full attention and you are able to clarify the issue ensuring that there are no misconceptions.

If you don't have/know the information they are asking for, admit it. There is nothing worse than trying to bluff your way through a conversation and it destroys the trust you have worked so hard to achieve.

It is important that you:

- say that you do not know everything but that you will find out and get back to them (giving a timeframe);
- follow up requests and find out all the relevant information before further discussions with the parents;
- put yourself in their shoes – how would you feel if this was your family, what are they actually asking for? – as by doing this you can empathise with an experience or situation and it becomes more real and important to you;
- you will not be able to solve every problem they have, so by working together as a team you can coach and mentor parents, enabling them to become more proactive and more in control of their particular issues.

CASE STUDY

Supporting parents/carers who are raising concerns

An irate parent arrived at school without an appointment and demanded to speak to (shout at) me. I calmly explained that I would be unable to meet with him if he continued to raise his voice. While leaving the reception area I asked for refreshments to be brought to the meeting room; that way another member of staff would be around if he didn't calm down (it is imperative to remember to always keep yourself safe). Once in the room I took charge of the conversation and set the ground rules for the meeting. I started by saying I could see

(Continued)

(Continued)

he was very upset, however, if he shouted at me or used inappropriate language I would be unable to continue to talk with him. Throughout this interaction I gave the impression of being calm and in control of the situation.

I spoke in a quieter voice than usual; that way he had to listen more intently to what I was saying. I asked him to tell me why he was upset so I had a full picture of the issues. As he spoke I listened to the first point and asked if I could answer. He felt the maths work was too easy for his son. I explained how we collected data throughout the term and set the work accordingly. I was able to show him a programme which automatically adjusts to the child's ability in response to teacher assessment.

He also felt his son needed more homework. To involve him in the decision making I gave him two options of how we could overcome this. Together we decided I would photocopy a batch of work that they could do at home together, along with learning all his times tables.

His final point was that he wanted his son to move to a 'higher' maths group; again I explained about making sure children were challenged but supported in their learning and that as a teacher I made judgement calls. I explained how confidence was an important factor in learning and sometimes it is better to be top of a group and gaining in confidence than to feel you are unable to keep up. I collected his son's maths books and assessment papers. On returning to the room I could show concrete evidence that supported my views.

Throughout the meeting I could see the father calming down and relaxing. When we reached the end of the discussion we set a date for a follow-up meeting to ensure that the concerns were resolved. As he left he thanked me for my time and apologised for the way he had initially behaved. I accepted the apology and said I understood how sometime emotions can get the better of us and I knew he only had the best interests of his son at heart. During the meeting I remained calm and confident while modelling the behaviour I was expecting to see from him.

 Key points to remember

- Always appear calm, in control and capable (even if you do not feel it).
- Always speak to a parent in private and NEVER discuss their child in front of other parents, staff or pupils.
- Ensure that colleagues are aware you are in a meeting with a parent/carer.

- It is important to remember safeguarding procedures when having discussions with parents. Some students may live at protected addresses or be in the care of the LA. It is imperative that information is kept confidential to protect students, parents and staff.
- Never prejudge parents; they usually only want what is best for their child.
- Listen to and hear parents; they have known the child longer than you.
- Place emphasis on it being a team approach and that parents are part of the team.
- Put yourself in their shoes. Ask yourself these three key questions: Would you feel the same way if it was your child? Would you react the same way if it was your child? What support would you want/ need if it was your child?
- Be consistent; always behave in the same way, regardless of how you are feeling or what is going on in your life. Remember that you are a professional.

Additional resources

As well as the resources you'll find at **www.sagepub.co.uk/martindenham** you should also take a look at the following:

Appreciate Diversity Month, www.sbhihelp.org/files/Diversity88Ways. pdf: This free-to-download resource provides 88 suggested activities you can use to celebrate diversity with pupils.

Stonewall, www.stonewall.org.uk: This organisation works to achieve equality and justice for lesbians, gay men and bisexual people. The website has a wealth of resources freely available to celebrate difference in schools. If you click on the 'At school' then 'Education resources' you will find a range of resources for use in schools from the early years to post 16.

Possible solutions

For the Reflective activity on p. 74

- Speak to the parent and explain the letter to them. If they agree they can sign it.
- Ask the parent how they would prefer information to be communicated to them.

CHAPTER 8

AUTISTIC SPECTRUM CONDITION

Jayne Littlewood and Claire Sewell

Key ideas explored in this chapter

- What is autistic spectrum condition (ASC)?
- The triad of impairment
- Current thinking in relation to the causes of ASC
- Approaches to teaching and learning for pupils with autism
- The inclusive classroom
- Understanding the pupil with autism

What is autistic spectrum condition (ASC)?

Autistic spectrum condition (ASC) is a complex lifelong developmental disability that may affect the way a person communicates and relates to others. The term 'spectrum' is often used because the condition varies from person to person. Some people with autism are able to live relatively independent lives but others may have accompanying learning disabilities that need a lifetime of specialist support. Those with autism may also experience over or under-sensitivity to sounds, touch, tastes, smells, lights or colours. It is common practice for many to distinguish between someone with autism and someone with a diagnosis of Asperger's syndrome. However, the new classification systems for identification of autism (DSM-V and ICD-11) do not make a distinction between autism and Aspergers, instead it is under the umbrella term 'ASC'.

Asperger syndrome is placed at the 'more able' end of the spectrum and includes those with average or above average intelligence with fewer speech difficulties. At the 'less able' end of the spectrum is Kanner's syndrome, sometimes referred to as 'classic autism'.

Kanner (1943) carried out eleven observational studies of pupils demonstrating what are known now to be autistic type behaviours. In the various cases he described how the pupils would not make eye contact and would like repetition and order. He further discussed how the pupils disliked change and preferred to be alone. The pioneering work of Lorna Wing (Wing and Gould, 1979) gave rise to the concept of the triad of impairments. This research identified a number of characteristics that when grouped together highlighted the key features we know now as autism.

An additional challenge for people with autism is in relation to their ability to comprehend the world using their senses. Research continues to ascertain the impact that sensory integration difficulties, also known as sensory sensitivity, can have on an individual with ASC but it is accepted that it can have a profound effect on a person's life (NAS, 2014).

The triad of impairment
communication
thinking flexibly / social imagination
social understanding.

Those with Autistic Spectrum Condition may have difficulties in three main areas: social communication; thinking flexibly and social imagination; and social understanding and relating. These are referred to as the 'triad of impairments' and are illustrated in Figure 8.1.

The additional impairment of the 'triad' is the sensory component, which is becoming increasingly understood as a result of research. Whilst the diagram has yet to be re-drawn incorporating this, the sensory impairments (e.g. hypo/hyper-sensitivity to touch, sound, taste, sight and smell) associated with autism are widely acknowledged.

Social communication
Literal understanding
Non-verbal

The pupils may encounter challenges in communicating effectively with others and may display the following:

- absence of desire to communicate;
- an inability to infer anything other than the literal meaning of spoken phrases;

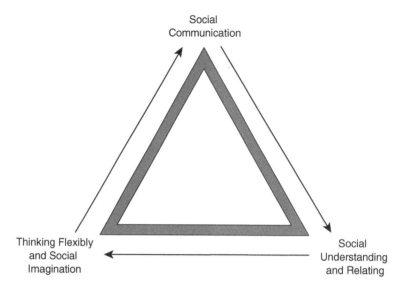

Figure 8.1   Triad of impairments (reproduced with permission from the TDA, 2008, © Crown Copyright)

- communicating for their own needs, rather than for social engagement;
- non-verbal, such as some pupils with autism, so you will need to find alternative ways to communicate, for example using the Picture Exchange Communication System (PECS®);
- asking the same question repeatedly even though it has been answered;
- talking about their own interests regardless of the level of response/interest;
- making factual comments when you are talking about something else.

Fixed thoughts
obsessive interests

Thinking flexibly and social imagination

The pupils you are teaching may have challenges in their flexible thinking regarding interests, routines, perspectives and rules. They may:

- not understand the points of view of others;
- be agitated and upset by a change in routine;
- have special interests which may appear obsessive;
- take everything literally and may not understand humour;
- be unable to generalise information.

Social understanding and relating

Non-verbal eyes
— social behaviours
— eye contact

The pupils may experience challenges in understanding how to behave and interact with others in school. They may:

- have difficulty understanding and using non-verbal behaviour, for example eye contact, facial expressions and gesture;
- stand too close to people or may not want to be near others;
- may appear uninterested and avoid eye contact;
- be unaware of the different ways to interact/touch teachers, friends and strangers;
- have a desire to have friends and relationships but may struggle to initiate and maintain these;
- touch other people inappropriately.

Additional difficulties

Pupils may also experience sensory difficulties, mental health difficulties and physical difficulties, including:

- over-sensitivity to some noises;
- a strong sense of personal space, which when encroached may cause distress;
- appearing to enjoy physical contact or alternatively not being touched;
- under-developed fine and gross motor skills, such as walking on tip toes and being clumsy;
- mood disturbances, for example anxiety, aggression or depression.

🖉 Key points to remember

- Those with autism do not always display any obvious physical characteristics, which can become a barrier to other people's understanding and appreciation of their needs.
- More recently sensory issues have been highlighted as a further area of difficulty. They may be over- or under-sensitive to sounds, touch, taste, smell, light and colour.
- Autism can affect individuals in many ways; each pupil will display unique behaviours that you need to understand.
- A person with autism may display different levels of prevalence of behaviour(s) within each or all of the three areas of the triad.

The following case study demonstrates the need for consistency when addressing the needs of a young adult with very difficult and at times unpredictable behaviour patterns.

CASE STUDY

Luca

Luca was a 17-year-old boy who received his diagnosis of autism when he was six. In terms of his cognitive development he was currently working at the age of a three-year-old pupil. When he was anxious he demonstrated negative behaviours such as biting, kicking and scratching as a means of communicating that something was not right. Over the past few years his behaviour had become increasingly challenging both at home and school. At home, his parents reported that he had started to hurt his younger siblings and they feel unable to cope.

What do you need to consider?

- Remember that all behaviours have a trigger and that as a professional it is your role to find out what this is so you can take steps to prevent them.
- It may be worth considering consulting with the multi-agency team as they may have additional information regarding the pupil, such as medical difficulties.
- The relationship between home and school is paramount in ensuring that a successful, consistent approach is maintained across both environments.
- Produce a behaviour plan in collaboration with all relevant parties. This will ensure that everyone involved in his care knows how to address his behaviours, creating a consistent approach.
- Regularly review the behaviour plan.
- The key concept is that 'good' behaviour is rewarded positively every single time with a reward that is meaningful and motivating to Luca.
- Signpost the family to support services and voluntary organisations, such as Contact a Family.

Current thinking in relation to the causes of ASCs

The exact causes of ASCs remain unknown. It has been correlated with an impairment of typical brain development before, during or after birth. Current research is suggesting that ASC has a strong genetic component but this is yet to be scientifically confirmed (Abrahams and Geschwind, 2008). Statistically, autism affects more males than females at a ratio of 4:1. The latest prevalence studies of autism suggested that 1.1 per cent of the population in the UK may have autism, which equates to 1 in every 100 people. Currently, there is no known 'cure' for the 700,000 individuals with autism in the UK (National Autistic Society, 2014), therefore we need to be focussing on their abilities rather than their disabilities and meeting their individual needs.

Approaches to teaching and learning for pupils with autism

It is important to remember that many pupils with autism are now being educated within a mainstream setting and thus any strategies implemented should also be beneficial to both the pupil with autism and the neuro-typical pupil. This section will consider the approaches to teaching and learning which may be adopted to make the school environment autism friendly. This is not to say all ideas have been highlighted or that it is possible to ensure that the classroom is completely autism friendly. However, gaining an overview of strategies which could be used will hopefully enable you to consider modifications which can be made to make learning a more positive experience for the pupil with autism.

Awareness of barriers to learning

In order to give all pupils the best possible chance to access high-quality teaching and learning opportunities, we need to consider three key areas: the classroom environment; the ability to communicate; and the 'readiness' of the pupil to participate and learn.

The classroom environment

For some pupils it is the classroom environment that is the barrier to learning. This chaotic and potentially unpredictable place does not usually meet the needs of a pupil with autism who appreciates order, routine and repetition. Any interference or change in the routine can lead to high levels of anxiety and an intensely emotional reaction.

The following case study demonstrates the need for a clear structure to be implemented and consistently adhered to.

CASE STUDY

James

James, aged three years, had a diagnosis of autism; he attended a mainstream nursery part time and spent his afternoons at home with his family. It became increasingly clear that James found the transition between the different parts of the day difficult, causing him to become upset and often extremely agitated.

How could James be supported in his different settings?

- Teaching James to recognise the symbols for the key elements of his day (home, nursery, car).
- Putting in place a visual timetable to support him when changes occur.
- Preparing him for changes in routine in advance of them happening by reinforcing the 'now' and 'then' elements of his visual timetable.
- Increasing the number of symbols he used as he became more accepting of the routines of his day.
- Sharing the visual timetable with the family once he is established in the nursery setting, and implementing it in the home.

The ability to communicate

Communication is the ability to give or be provided with information which occurs vicariously through displays of body language and explicitly through talk, both of which a pupil with autism can find difficult. A classroom where communication is unsupported could be deemed a barrier to learning for a person who can find social communication and interaction very difficult.

The 'readiness' of the pupil to participate and learn

The need to be 'ready to participate' and 'ready to work' can also be a barrier to learning if the pupil is experiencing sensory integration dysfunction. This affects the ability to process sensory input (sound, sight, touch, movement, body awareness and the pull of gravity). In order to support a pupil to become ready to access learning, the co-ordinated support of the parents/carers and other professionals will be needed.

The following case study reflects the significance of supporting a pupil in order that they are able to work to the best of their ability.

CASE STUDY

Duncan

Duncan, aged six, had a diagnosis of autism with related learning difficulties. His receptive and expressive language was very limited, although he could make his basic needs known using symbols. In order for Duncan to be 'ready for work', he needs a particular book to be positioned in a place of his choosing. If this isn't allowed, he is likely to become very anxious and display very challenging, often aggressive behaviour. As professionals our aim is to decrease his dependency on the book.

How could you support Duncan?

- Ensure that Duncan is allowed to put the book in a mutually agreeable place.
- Make an individual schedule (visual timetable) using symbols showing him 'work' then 'book' time. He must complete his work activity before being allowed his book.
- Use an electronic timer to show Duncan that when work time is finished he will get the book. Keep this at a very short time span initially and increase it as Duncan becomes more accepting of this approach.
- Over time increase the work expectations and length of time before allowing book time. Gradually work towards the book not being on the table at work time but in a place accessible to Duncan once work has finished either at the end of the morning period or at the end of the school day.

The inclusive classroom

An inclusive classroom needs to be a welcoming, safe and nurturing environment where the staff team acknowledge and respect the needs, the abilities and the identity of all pupils. This respectful and caring approach promotes holistic learning and development. When choosing the most appropriate strategy to try you must remember that autism is a spectrum condition. It is not always easy to put all the ideas into practice within the confines of the school and classroom. However, when a practitioner aims to meet the needs of all within it, the outcomes are nearly always positive.

Outlined below are some useful strategies and techniques that can be used to support a pupil with autism in both a mainstream classroom and/or a special educational provision.

A structured environment

One of the most effective ways of supporting pupils with autism is to create a well-structured and supportive environment. This can take many forms depending on the ability and/or the age of the pupil. For example, for younger or less able pupils a visual timetable using photographs, pictures or symbols set out over a given period (a morning or afternoon session) showing each different activity in the context of the day can be helpful. Once the activity has finished the symbol can be removed to a 'finished pouch' and the next activity on the schedule can take place. This enables the pupil to see and continue to check on events and activities, and gives them a sense of security in the knowledge that their day has structure.

 Key points to remember

- For older or more able pupils, a written timetable which they can manage themselves by crossing out each activity once completed can be very useful.
- Transitions between activities need to be clearly demarcated and defined in order that pupils know when one activity is about to end and a change is about to occur.

 Reflective activity

You have been asked to work in a class with two pupils who have not yet received a diagnosis but whose behaviours are typical of a pupil with autism. The class teacher has minimal experience of autism and asks for your help. What suggestions and advice might you offer?

Communication approaches

It can be a challenge to gain and maintain eye contact with a pupil with autism. Therefore you need to find an approach that works for you and the pupil whereby you know they are listening to you.

- Say the pupil's name clearly and repeatedly so that they know you are directly talking to them.
- Time needs to be allowed for both the pupil to process the fact that you are speaking to them and for them to understand what you are asking them to do.
- Use 'in-task schedules'. Often a pupil with autism will not understand that a lesson may involve more than one activity. An in-task schedule will show the pupil the different activities that will take place during a specific lesson; for example, during a literacy lesson use symbols to show 'story', 'talking', 'game', 'writing' and 'finished'.
- Visual supports are used to aid communication between adults and pupils; they remain after the verbal cue has been given and act as a reminder of expectations or can be used to inform another person of a need.
- Visual tools can also enhance learning (e.g. objects of reference such as a swimming costume to represent a swimming lesson).

Consistency and positive behaviour strategies

In establishing and consistently maintaining boundaries pupils learn safely what expectations adults have of them. Often pupils with autism find it difficult to understand how to behave and interact with other people; they need to be told/shown what is expected. It is important that they understand the rules of the classroom.

 Key points to remember

- Display classroom rules; these should be displayed visually, and frequently revisited to ensure a clear understanding of boundaries and expectations.
- Allow time for reflection and activities of the pupil's choosing within the structure of their day and include this in their schedule. This may mean allowing them to spend time on activities which often do not appear to be educational. For example, for a pupil who is obsessive about washing machines you may allow them 10 minutes at the end of a session to go and sit in the laundry room watching/listening to the spin cycle.

Understanding the pupil with autism

In order for you to be an integral part of the classroom environment you need to know the nuances of each pupil that make them individual. Therefore you need to engage in professional dialogue with staff members to gain an overview of the pupils within the group. A quick and easy approach to this is the 'pupil passport', which provides information on their particular needs and interests.

Key points to remember

- It is important that you know what pupils' behaviour triggers are so you don't increase their anxiety levels unknowingly.
- If a pupil does become over-anxious, disruptive or challenging it is important you remain calm and allow experienced staff to manage the situation.
- Tell pupils what they are good at to build their confidence and highlight their successes to their peers. Additionally, for the pupil with autism these strategies reinforce positive behaviours.
- Remembering to reinforce positive behaviours is vital as it demonstrates the expected behaviour, thus encouraging the pupil to make the right choice.

Through implementing the above approaches, you can enable the pupil with autism alongside his/her peers to begin to rely upon you to support them in a place that would otherwise appear chaotic and unpredictable. This will allow the individual with autism to begin to make sense of their environment. This will then open up opportunities to interact, communicate and understand what is going on around them.

What pupils with autism would like you to know

- I need to have the same structure and approach to learning in any classroom that I am in.
- I need to know what is expected of me so I can be prepared; a visual timetable will let me know what is going to happen.

- I need you to recognise my anxieties and inform others because I may not be able to.
- I deal with each of my anxieties in a different way, and new staff need to know what helps me in each situation.
- Stay calm with me, even if I do not stay calm with myself as I can't always understand my feelings.
- I need you to say my name before you speak to me; please wait until you have my attention.
- Give me time to respond and interact in my own way and allow me to make choices and decisions for myself; I may need support with this.
- I often need periods of time away from you and from demands; I may need times during the day to do my rhythmic activities freely.
- I respond well to rewards for doing what you ask.

An autism toolbox of strategies/resources

There are numerous strategies/resources that are available to support those with autism to work towards the same outcome, which is to promote their independence thus reducing their dependency on others. These are only a selection; however, more information can be found out about each on the websites as indicated at the end of the chapter.

- Emotional regulators such as Blu-Tac®, a rubber snake, ribbons to aid emotional regulation: Social Communication, Emotional Regulation and Transactional Support (SCERTS®).
- Ear defenders to deaden noise.
- Intensive interaction, for learning the early and fundamental communication attainments.
- Use of Social Stories™ to help pupils understand different situations, events and expectations.
- Motivators linked to the pupil's special interest; this could be anything, including particular foods, toys or activities.
- Pictures, symbols – in fact any visual aid needed by your pupils.
- Access to a range of technologies available such as iPads and apps.
- Ask for advice and guidance from the team you are working with.

The following case study demonstrates how information and communications technology (ICT) can be used to support pupils with communication difficulties.

CASE STUDY

Maisie

Maisie, aged 14, has high-level receptive language skills but because of other learning difficulties she had no expressive language at all. She was able to use symbols at a basic level to answer questions in class and also used PECS® to communicate her basic needs. Maisie was often frustrated as she found it very difficult to make herself understood. However, staff worked closely with a SLT and with the introduction of an iPad Maisie was able to communicate and express herself for the first time. Her anxiety levels notably decreased as a result of her competency in using the iPad.

Next steps for Maisie

- Organise the iPad symbols into categories for easy access and model how to find the different symbols which Maisie may need.
- Increase the number of symbols that Maisie is familiar with by demonstrating using practical activities which are meaningful and functional to her.
- Continue to develop her use of the iPad in the local community to communicate in real-life situations, such as ordering food in a restaurant.
- Ensure that staff training in the use of the iPad is current and relevant.
- Keep up to date with current technologies and ensure that the most appropriate resource is being used to meet Maisie's needs.

Additional resources

As well as the resources you'll find at **www.sagepub.co.uk/martindenham** you should also take a look at the following:

The following websites are recommended as being excellent sources of information in relation to developing your own knowledge, skills and understanding of how to support individuals with ASCs using a range of approaches:

- www.scerts.com
- www.teacch.com
- www.autism.org.uk

If you are looking for support with communication issues, then accessing the following websites would be recommended:

- www.pecs-unitedkingdom.com
- www.makaton.org
- www.thegraycentre.org/social-stories

For information on intensive interaction, visit www.intensiveinteraction. co.uk: This website will provide you with comprehensive information about intensive interaction, including signposting to conferences, courses and books.

For general information, access The National Autistic Society at www. autism.org.uk: This website will give you guidance in supporting children in your class to develop an understanding of autistic type behaviours and difficulties.

The Circle of Friends: This aims to promote inclusion and interaction, and is particularly useful. The approach supports the class in developing strategies and practical solutions to help the individual with autism to feel a part of the class group.

Research Autism: Improving the Quality of Life, http://researchautism. net: A website is aimed at anyone with an interest in autism. It provides up-to-date, scientifically reliable information about autism. It also provides information about the issues facing individuals with autism and a wide range of interventions used to manage autism and co-occurring conditions.

CHAPTER 9

SPEECH, LANGUAGE AND COMMUNICATION NEEDS (SLCN)

Jan Patterson and Chris Roberts

Key ideas explored in this chapter

- The stages in learning to communicate linked to performance levels (P scales)
- The use of augmentative and alternative communication (AAC)
- Communication methods used to engage and interact with pupils who have PMLD or SLD
- Eye gaze and the use of the E-Tran (eye transfer) frame
- Picture Exchange Communication System (PECS)®
- Signing to support communication
- Symbols to support communication
- Communication grids and books: using core vocabulary
- Voice output communication aids (VOCA)
- The use of technology
- Developing communication in the classroom (for those with significant needs)
- Supporting pupils with speech, language and communication needs (SLCN)

It would be useful to familiarise yourself with P scales before reading this chapter. P scales are a common way of assessing pre-level 1 pupils and will be referred to in this chapter; you can see these at www.gov.uk.

The stages in learning to communicate linked to performance levels (P scales)

Pupils who are working at the earliest stages of development (P1) are described as being at the 'pre-intentional' level of communication. Their responses, which may reflect their feelings, are usually automatic and often reflex. Behaviours, movements, sounds and facial expressions need to be observed and analysed by sensitive adults and given meaning.

The approaches used for pupils at the early stages of development (some of which are discussed in Chapter 8) include: intensive interaction; Tacpac®; sensory experiences; co-active (adult assisted) exploration of objects; and establishing regular, explicit routines with 'objects of reference' as cues to activities.

Most pupils at these early stages should have input from a specialist SLT, who will provide specific advice and may be available to plan jointly with the adults supporting the pupil. Pupils at these stages need extensive and sensitive individual adult support to ensure that they have a 'voice'. Many of them will have profound and multiple learning difficulties, including physical disabilities. They are often described as 'hard to reach' as they do not yet have the means to make their needs known. It takes perseverance, patience and a lot of time to enable the pupils to express themselves, but it is worth every second!

Over time the pupils may develop the ability to anticipate what will happen in their regular routines and interactions (P2). They begin to show recognition of familiar objects, by facial expression and body movement (the time this takes will vary). The approaches above continue to be appropriate at this stage; however the, pupils will become more active vocally and physically and their responses will show some understanding. They may give more eye contact and the adult should begin to decrease the support in the exploration of objects and sensory materials. It is important to maintain the familiar routines and objects and to name them.

 Key point to remember

- Use the pupil's name repeatedly to focus their attention.

Pupils may then develop intentional responses and joint attention (P3). They will begin to indicate what they want, by looking, vocalising or possibly gesturing. At this stage they may learn to choose between two objects. They will need several opportunities to develop their responses throughout each day, using the approaches mentioned earlier. Adults will need to provide lots of turn taking, repetitive games and further exploration of everyday objects in context.

Pupils at the next stages of development begin to understand simple words (comprehension) and those with speech may begin to copy and use some words (expression, P4). It is helpful for adults to use key words when communicating with pupils at this level and accompany their speech with signing (Makaton® or BSL) to give visual cues. This supports the development of understanding of key words and focuses their attention on the speaker. It may be useful to introduce photographs and/or symbols at this stage as concrete representations of activities to further support pupils' understanding of language. Pupils then need to learn an increasing number of words. It is important to use repetition of words that are within their everyday experiences. Parents and carers need to be informed of the focus in class so they can reinforce the learning at home. Adults narrating or describing pupils' actions, to which the pupil is attending and/or sharing, is a very effective approach to developing vocabulary and understanding.

As pupils develop their vocabulary they can put words together. However, they often pick up common phrases as single words like 'all gone', 'no more' and may need more support to form phrases to comment or describe, for example 'Daddy gone', 'car gone'.

The use of augmentative and alternative communication (AAC)

Augmentative and alternative communication (AAC) is an umbrella term used to describe the communication methods used to support (augment) speaking, or instead (alternative) of speaking. Augmentative strategies used to support speech include: gesture, facial expression, eye pointing, Makaton® and other signing and symbol systems, and writing. All may be used in place of or alongside speech to support expressive communication, perhaps when a pupil's speech is unclear. They can be used by an adult to support pupils' understanding of spoken language.

There are a wide range of techniques and approaches that replace speech, such as word boards, communication boards and books and voice output communication aids (VOCAs). Signing can also be an alternative strategy; British Sign Language (BSL) may be used by those with hearing difficulties. Many pupils with SLCN will need some form of AAC and will benefit from the use of visual supports for their understanding. This is usually developed with a SLT, particularly if the pupil needs an alternative means of communication.

Key points to remember

- Repeat and expand the pupil utterances providing a model for developing sentence structure.
- Adjust your language to make your instructions clear and concise.
- Use familiar key words alongside Makaton® signs or gestures.
- Give time for pupils to process what you have said and respond. If they do not respond check that they have understood, repeat what you have said or ask a simple question.
- Provide more support if they have not understood what you have said.

CASE STUDY

Brady

Brady, aged four, arrived at his new school from his nursery where he had been described by staff as being overly dependent. His previous report stated that he often displayed violent behaviours and was unable to communicate with his peers or staff. He made some sounds and obviously expected the adults to know what he wanted. He cried for his mother most days and did not take part in any activities that were offered to him. He would not join in group story time, preferring to wander around the classroom on his own.

The classroom Brady joined catered for pupils with a wide range of learning difficulties. On his first day he was greeted by name by the three members of staff who signed and said 'Hello Brady'; he smiled and copied the sign and vocalised in greeting. The member of staff from the nursery who had accompanied him on his first day was astounded and said he had never communicated with them like that in a whole year. When shown the visual timetable, he joined the morning group session. He sat on his chair and watched the other eight children in the group respond to the register saying and signing 'Yes'; when his name was called he made an attempt to sign and vocalise. He was able to join the group session for 10 minutes. He also made attempts to join in some of the songs alongside his peers. He was given a 'welcome wave' by staff and pupils as part of the group session and a sticker for sitting well on his first day.

This simple explicit structure with adults using simple clear language supported by signs and symbols enabled Brady to achieve on his first day something he had not managed in the previous context. He never displayed violent behaviours towards his peers again.

Communication methods used to engage and interact with pupils who have PMLD or SLD

In this section methods of communication will be described that can be used to support pupils with either PMLD or SLD. Most, but not all, of the pupils will be pre-verbal with expressive communication levels falling between P3 and P8.

In most schools where pupils have specific communication needs there will have been involvement and input from a SLT. In some schools there may even be speech therapists on the staff who can advise and work with pupils on a regular basis. The more the teaching practitioner can work alongside the speech therapist the better.

   Key points to remember

- Get to know the SLT in the school and find out their role and responsibilities.
- Ask about the communication strategies being used and why.
- Plan lessons with input from the SLT, or better still jointly with the SLT.

Eye gaze and the use of the E-Tran (eye transfer) frame

Once it has been established that eye contact can be made between pupil and practitioner, the next step is to teach the pupil that choices can be made by 'gazing' with intention at either an object, a picture or a symbol. Clearly, by holding apart two objects and asking 'which one', a simple choice may be made by looking at the preferred object. This is developed by holding two motivating pictures; again a choice is made by looking at the preferred picture. The reward is of course to give the pupil their chosen item depicted by the picture. This could, for instance, be a toy, a story or a snack.

Further progression is made by using symbols, either referring to an object or to a word. Symbols with contrasting words will have most impact: Yes/No; More/Stop. Obviously the meaning of the words needs to be taught and reinforced.

A very useful tool for working with pupils who are starting to understand eye gaze (also referred to as 'eye pointing') is the E-Tran frame. This is a simple device, which can be either homemade or purchased online or from catalogues. Basically it is a rectangular piece of perspex with a window in the middle, as shown in Figure 9.1.

Figure 9.1 The E-Tran frame

In its simplest form, single symbols are placed on the corners of the frame. The practitioner (communication partner) faces the pupil and holds the frame up between them. Usually in response to a question the pupil will look at the symbol that they want to say. As the pupil becomes more skilled, the frame can become more complex and symbols may be added in the middle of each side (it is common practice to use either the middle vertical or horizontal plane for Yes/No).

The method can be made more complex using colour or number coding systems so that more items/symbols can be accessed. It is common for advanced users to access the alphabet using an E-Tran frame, allowing them to spell out words. There are very sophisticated eye tracking computers on the market. These are aimed at the high-functioning AAC user and are generally not seen in the classroom for PMLD and complex needs pupils.

Picture Exchange Communication System (PECS)®

PECS® is a form of AAC produced by Pyramid Educational Consultants, Inc. It is a method to teach young children and adults with communication impairment a way to develop and establish functional communication.

The essence of PECS® is that the user learns to spontaneously exchange a picture of a desired object or activity and in return receives the object or activity. This is the first of six stages; once making a spontaneous request is established, the pupils learns to discriminate pictures. The level of functional communication skills the pupil could achieve might also include responsive requests, and responsive and spontaneous comments.

In the classroom for pupils with PMLD or communication difficulties, PECS® is used to encourage and develop communication. The first role of the communication partner is to identify motivators, for example, things that the pupil wants. These may be favourite toys, activities or quite often food or drink. The pupil reaching for an object shows that they are motivated by it; this is the time to teach the exchange of a picture (this may be a photograph of the object or a symbol to represent the object).

In this first phase the pupil will give the communication partner a picture of an object in exchange for the object. It should be noted that the communication partner must not thank the pupil for the picture; they should reinforce the request by handing over the item and saying the name of the item or saying a simple phrase such as 'I want ...'. At this early stage two people are needed to teach the exchange: the communication partner plus another to help with the physical direction of picking up and handing over the card (this person sits silently behind the pupil). This can be a lengthy process which requires patience on the part of the communication partner.

Once this is established the next phase is for the pupil to draw the attention of the communication partner. They may travel to the communication partner to exchange the message or if the pupil has mobility difficulties, which will be common in pupils with PMLD, they can be taught how to draw the attention of the communication partner. This could be by ringing a bell, or pressing a button with a recorded message saying 'Come here please', or indeed by physical contact or possibly vocalising, a bit like the child shouting for something that they want.

The next phase is discrimination between symbols. During this phase the pupil is taught discrimination of symbols and how to select the symbol which depicts a desired item. The pupil may be given more than one picture. They have to choose the correct picture for the item that they want; if they give the wrong picture, then the object corresponding to the picture should be given. There are specific reinforcement strategies and error correction procedures used during this phase to ensure that the pupil discriminates among pictures.

It should be noted that the pupil could reach their limit at any of the three phases described above. Achieving any one should be considered a real achievement for the pupil and may well prove significant in the quality of their life.

Reflective activity

Working in a mixed ability group with a range of learning difficulties, staff inform you that one pupil has a PECS® file. What would you do? (Some suggestions are given at the end of the chapter.)

CASE STUDY

Use of PECS® to promote communication

Connor, 11 years old, had autism with SLD (working within P4) together with some challenging behaviours.

Connor had no speech other than the occasional 'grunts' that did not seem to have any identifiable meaning. He had not used PECS® previously. Significantly, Connor was very motivated by food so it was decided to use the PECS® system to enable him to request drinks and snacks. Progress was quite rapid and he was soon able to make a picture exchange, first for a drink and then for a biscuit. He soon learnt that different pictures had different meanings and a choice of drink was introduced, either orange juice or blackcurrant juice. He was then introduced to the concept of requesting a toy using picture exchange, which progressed to choosing a specific toy. His main motivator remained having a drink or snack. He would go to his card board and collect the drink card and push it at whoever was in the room to make the request. He also learnt the symbol for toilet, which was particularly useful. His board has just three cards on it: toilet, drink and biscuit. These were usually chosen accurately and reflected his needs at the time. If he chose a drink, then he would be offered a choice of drink.

Like anyone learning a new skill he also learnt how to exploit it. If he was fed up with working and wanted to leave the room he would show his toilet card; he was then taken to the toilet but would just look at it and return to class. He would collect his snack cards at times that were not always appropriate and learnt that he did not always get his request. Care must be taken with this approach not to de-motivate, so if a snack is not immediately available he would be told 'later' (when snacks must be made available). An additional bonus with this strategy was that Connor also learnt how to sign 'Please' and 'Thank you' when getting his snack, which really pleased his parents.

The next three phases in the development of PECS® are described below. These will be applicable to pupils either working at or progressing to the upper P levels (P4–P6).

During phase 4 the pupil is taught sentence structure in order to make requests by using expressions such as 'I want ... ', as seen in Figure 9.2.

Figure 9.2   Using symbols to form a sentence

During phase 5 the pupil is taught to respond to questions such as 'What do you want?'. The goal of this phase is for the child to respond 'I want ...' regardless of whether the item is present.

In phase 6 of the PECS® protocol the pupil is taught to respond to questions as well as to spontaneously comment on items, people or activities present in their environment. By the end of phase 6 the pupil can now make spontaneous requests and respond to questions such as 'What do you want?' with 'I want ...' and to respond to questions such as 'What do you hear, smell etc.' with a sentence 'I can hear ...'.

Clearly, for a pupil to be able to communicate their wants and needs throughout the day, particularly at this higher level, can become very important for their quality of life. When teaching pupils the phases the teacher may see commercially produced PECS® communication books being used in the classroom, but is just as likely to see teacher-produced cards and boards. It should be noted that each pupil must have their own book regardless of who has produced it.

 Key points to remember

- It is important that if PECS® is used as a communication method it is used consistently, so the pupil understands that communication serves a purpose, and that the protocol is followed for optimal success.
- It is likely that the pupils you are working with will already be working at the appropriate phase. Progression to the next phase would normally be done in collaboration with the SLT or a teacher experienced and trained in the use of PECS®.

Signing to support communication

There are essentially two types of AAC: unaided and aided. Unaided refers to those methods that do not require any additional equipment or resources over and above what the pupil possesses: their face, hands and body. With these a message can be conveyed with facial expression, body language, gesture, pointing and signing. Usually the use of sign language is associated with those with hearing impairments. However, in the classroom for pupils with complex needs, signs and gestures provide visual reinforcement to what is being said. There are several signing systems in use, including BSL, which is the system most commonly used by those with hearing impairments. Makaton® and Signalong are both based on BSL and are commonly used to support communication of people with leaning difficulties.

Both Makaton® and Signalong are supposed to be used at the same time as speech, to aid understanding and to allow simple self-expression (sign supported English). For those pupils without speech, simple signing can get a message across for them. Used in isolation or in combination with symbols and perhaps vocalising, pupils can have a voice.

When signing is being used as part of an AAC system it is important that you speak as you sign; for a complete communication system there may also be some modelling using communication cards. Together this will provide visual reinforcement to what is being said; pupils with very severe speech and learning difficulties will have problems understanding and remembering what has been said to them. The combination of speech, signing and symbols can provide pupils with all the clues to support their understanding.

Key point to remember

- There are limiting factors in the use of signing: the motor skills of the pupil may not allow for some of the movement, resulting in an inaccurate sign that is unreadable.

Symbols to support communication

The use of symbols is commonplace in developing communication. There are a number of commercially available symbol packages, each with their different merits. The commonly used symbol systems, and the ones most likely to be encountered by the trainee teacher, are Blissymbols™, Makaton®, PICS for PECS® images, Picture Communication Symbols (PCS™), and Widgit Symbols (WLS™).

The teacher may go into one provision and find that picture communication is being taught using one communication system, then move to another provision and find another system in use. Individual schools will have investigated the symbols available and made the decision of

The Picture Communication Symbols ©1981–2011 by Mayer-Johnson LLC. All Rights Reserved Worldwide. Used with permission Boardmaker® is a trademark of Mayer-Johnson LLC.

Figure 9.3   A symbol fan used to express happy/sad/confused feelings

which symbol type best suits their need. Whatever the system chosen, the symbols will need to be taught to the pupils. Some of the symbols are easily guessed, others are not. The purpose of symbols is to convey a word or sometimes a short phrase in symbol form, and then be used to aid communication in place of speech or writing. The symbol may be a direct representation of the word or may be somewhat abstract; different symbol packages will vary in this regard.

The symbol fan is used for pupils to express happy/sad/confused (see Figure 9.3). You need to consider the standardisation of symbols used to represent specific words. In many of the symbol systems the symbols can vary, so check which ones are being used in your context.

Communication grids and books: using core vocabulary

In the world of AAC, the use of communication grids and books represents the 'low-tech' solution to aiding communication. Communication grids and books are an extension to the use of single symbols.

In one now commonly used system, *Making and Using a Communication Book*, published by ACE Centre (http://acecentre.org.uk/developing-and-using-a-communication-book), a communication book is produced for the pupil. When you open the book the left-hand page

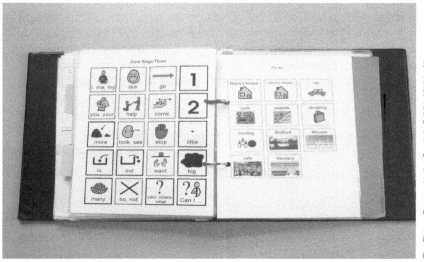

Figure 9.4 Example of a communication book

is a grid of 'core vocabulary symbols' and on the right-hand page is a grid of 'topic symbols' (see Figure 9.4). The pupil is taught to use one or more of the core vocabulary symbols with the topic symbol to make a simple statement. In this system there are five stages of 'core vocabulary', which get progressively more complex. The 'topic' pages are created with the specific pupil in mind and may have some specific motivating symbols or indeed pictures; for instance, there may be pictures of family and familiar places. As well as the pupil-specific pages there are also generic pages; colours, activities and foods, for example.

Clearly, the level of core vocabulary used to make each book is dependent on the pupil's ability. When making a book the core vocabulary remains a constant and although many of the topic pages can be generic it is important that some of the pages are specific, therefore motivating, for the pupil. Communication books then have a standard format that is easily reproduced, but also have that element of individuality. Pupils will need to be taught how to use their book; it should be readily available at all times so will need to be of a convenient size.

To aid phrase and sentence construction colour coding is often used, either as a border for the symbols or as a block colour on the grid. Any colour system can be used with graphic symbols as long as it is consistent. Recommended colours are given in Table 9.1.

Communication grids may be used successfully in isolation. For example, a grid could be produced for a specific activity and then given to the pupils to aid their communication whilst undertaking the activity. Grids can be created to give pupils a voice when playing simple games. Grids can be made to teach the vocabulary in a story. Pupils can then use the grid to answer questions or predict what is going to happen next.

When using communication grids it is very important that the communication partner models the use of the grid whilst talking to the pupil. Careful observation must be made to observe the pupil's communication response. The communication partner should reinforce their symbol by pointing with speech and clarifying what the

Table 9.1 Recommended colours for use in sentence construction

People	Yellow
Verbs	Green
Descriptions	Blue
Nouns	Orange
Social	Pink
Miscellaneous	White

pupil has 'said' with speech. It is very easy to miss pupils pointing to vocabulary on the grid if distracted. Pupils will only be motivated to use the grids if they feel that they are being 'listened to'.

Voice output communication aids (VOCA)

VOCAs represent the 'high-tech' solution to aiding communication, and range from the relatively cheap and simple to the complex and expensive. All have been designed to help give voice to pupils who are either unable to speak or who cannot communicate effectively through speech. All produce spoken words to help the user get their message across; depending on the complexity of the machine, this may be a single word or a complete sentence (see Figures 9.5 and 9.6).

In the classroom for pupils with PMLD/SLD it is likely that the VOCA for general use encountered by the trainee teacher will be relatively

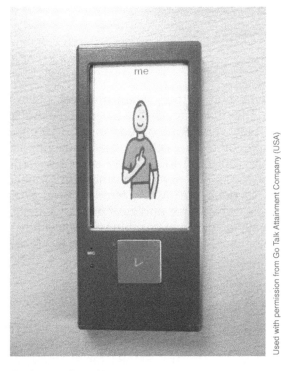

Used with permission from Go Talk Attainment Company (USA)

The Picture Communication Symbols ©1981–2011 by Mayer-Johnson LLC. All Rights Reserved Worldwide. Used with permission Boardmaker® is a trademark of Mayer-Johnson LLC.

Figure 9.5 Single-word VOCA

Figure 9.6   Complete sentence VOCA

simple. From the single button that, when pressed, plays a recorded word or phrase, to the machine that has multiple buttons which, when pressed, may play various recorded words or phrases relevant to the individual pupil, or to the activity that the pupil is undertaking. The multiple cells (buttons) VOCA may accept a communication grid as described above. As the pupil's communication needs become more sophisticated, so does the VOCA. Multi-layered programmable machines are available, which give endless communication opportunities. These are normally single-user machines and will have been programmed with the individual pupil in mind, specific to his or her needs.

The use of technology

The classroom computer can be used very successfully as a communication tool when used in conjunction with an interactive whiteboard. Depending on the available software, SMART for example, it is possible to create buttons on the whiteboard. Speech can be added to the buttons so that when they are pressed by the pupils you have effectively created a large VOCA. With the appropriate software the buttons can be moved around by the pupils to create simple phrases or sentences.

Probably one of the most exciting developments for the AAC user is the tablet computer. There are now many communication apps available, some of which are free.

Developing communication in the classroom (for those with significant needs)

For pupils with significant communication needs, a teaching approach that promotes communication through a combination of signing, PECS®, communication symbol books and the use of high- and low-tech communication aids can be very successful.

The principle of 'engineering the environment' when used in conjunction with the above can be very powerful. In other words, creating classroom situations where pupils are really motivated to communicate. This can be achieved by using missing or incorrect items, omitted steps, incomplete or mischievous actions, and interruptions – pausing and waiting for a response from the pupils – taking advantage of all opportunities for communication between peers as well as between pupils and adults. All of this can be achieved using stories, drama, music and games.

Supporting pupils with speech, language and communication needs (SLCN)

Every pupil with SLCN needs particular attention by the teacher as they will not be able to learn effectively until they understand and can give meaning to what is happening in the classroom. This may result in pupils displaying inappropriate behaviours or becoming increasingly withdrawn, falling further and further behind their peers.

It is important to establish the pupils' level of understanding of language before you begin to teach them, as this must have an impact on your approach. Always use current strategies that are familiar to the pupils. Think carefully about how your sentences are structured. Modelling simple language is crucial for pupils working between P3 and P8, as they are still learning what communication is and how it works. Take every opportunity to narrate the pupils' actions and reinforce their understanding by using photos of the activities to make books to read and share with them.

Key points to remember

- Never respond negatively to pupils' attempts to communicate or use spoken language.
- Consider using photographs or symbols as prompts for pupils who experience challenges with verbal instructions.
- Promote confidence.
- Always acknowledge them and repeat the correct model.
- Be engaging and enthusiastic; 'teacher presence' is crucial when working with pupils with this level of need.
- Try to keep your spoken language at a level which the pupil can understand; if they are only able to use single words, don't use complex sentences.

For the teachers entering a classroom with pupils with the complex needs described above for the first time it can be very daunting. Don't worry, there will always be other adults ready and willing to support and guide you. Go in with a smile and an open mind, just sit down with the pupils and talk with them.

Additional resources

As well as the resources you'll find at **www.sagepub.co.uk/martindenham** you should also take a look at the following:

Communication Matters, www.communicationmatters.org.uk: This organisation is dedicated to ensuring that every child has the right to a voice. The website has has links to an e-library, publications and online forums. Here you will find a wealth of information regarding AAC for both teacher and user.

The Schools Network Ltd (SSAT): This was commissioned by the Department for Education (DfE) to develop resources to support the teaching of pupils with PMLD. There are nine briefing sheets on particular areas of exceptionality with a briefing sheet, information sheets and classroom support guidance. These can be found at http://complexld.ssatrust.org.uk/ and is highly recommended.

The Makaton Charity, www.makaton.org: The website provides a useful overview of the benefits of using Makaton® to aid communication. There are also links to research, training and an online shop.

Possible solutions

For the Reflective activity on p. 99

This chapter will have given you a brief insight into what PECS® is about but will by no means have made you an expert. Ask the class teacher (or support staff) who works with the pupil about the phase of PECS® that the pupil is working at. If you have a lesson plan in mind, discuss it with the PECS® partner to ensure that suitable symbols are available for your activity. If possible ask to work alongside the PECS® partner and pupil so that you can see what the pupil is able to achieve. Your long-term aim should be to try to arrange some PECS® training for yourself.

CHAPTER 10

SPECIFIC LEARNING DIFFICULTIES (SpLD), DYSLEXIA, DYSPRAXIA AND DYSCALCULIA

Helen Irving and Sarah Martin-Denham

Key ideas explored in this chapter

- What is a specific learning difficulty (SpLD)?
- What is dyslexia?
- What is the impact of dyslexia on pupils?
- What are the indicators and how are pupils assessed for dyslexia?
- Scotopic sensitivity or Irlen Syndrome
- Making your classroom dyslexia friendly
- The particular needs of pupils with dyspraxia
- The particular needs of pupils with dyscalculia

What is a specific learning difficulty (SpLD)?

SpLD is an umbrella term used to describe a range of often co-occurring difficulties such as dyslexia, dyspraxia, dyscalculia, ADD, ADHD and auditory processing disorder – genetic conditions which can occur regardless of intelligence. The British Dyslexia Association, 2014 describes a SpLD as a condition which is affected by the way information is learned and processed.

What is dyslexia?

There are many definitions of dyslexia which have been created for over a hundred years by psychologists, researchers, neurologists and educationalists. One of the most explanatory definitions is:

> Dyslexia is a neurologically-based, often familial disorder which interferes with the acquisition and processing of language. Varying in degrees of severity, it is manifested by difficulties in receptive language, including phonological processing, in reading, writing, spelling, handwriting and sometimes in arithmetic. Although dyslexia is life long individuals with dyslexia frequently respond successfully to timely and appropriate intervention. (International Dyslexia Association, 2008)

The word dyslexia comes from 'dys', meaning difficulty, and 'lexis', meaning the totality of words in a language.

Approximately 10 per cent of the population have mild to severe dyslexia and 4 per cent are considered severely dyslexic. Many of these remain undiagnosed. However, once you have highlighted that a pupil is having difficulties it is important to make timely and appropriate interventions. All of the strategies that will be outlined in this chapter will be appropriate and beneficial for all children. All teachers will have, and do have, pupils with dyslexia (from mild to severe) in their classes but perhaps are not aware.

What is the impact of dyslexia on pupils?

Imagine living in a world where you can see, hear and talk confidently to those around you but when you have to read or write anything you feel as though you have been transported to another planet in which you cannot communicate or understand anything.

Positives of dyslexia

Many people with dyslexia are successful in their careers because of their differences and strengths. As teachers you need to celebrate their unique abilities and promote self-belief. Pupils with dyslexia simply have different learning preferences. It is necessary to acknowledge their strengths and utilise them to scaffold their learning. You must to give them the tools they need to excel.

CASE STUDY

My dyslexia

By Adam George Best

After many years struggling through the education system regardless of numerous concerns being raised by my parents, I was finally diagnosed with dyslexia following a full screening by an educational psychologist in higher education. This was met with mixed emotions. Although there was some relief that there was a reason for my difficulties in spelling, writing and reading (speed), there was increasing frustration and distress. It was difficult to come to terms with this new 'label', especially after being told that my difficulties were definitely not dyslexia related (in my secondary school). A subsequent concern was that as this diagnosis came within my first year at the University of Sunderland, I wondered if I was going to be able to keep up with the academic demands of higher education. Ultimately, there was an overall feeling that my ability was capped, that this dyslexia would stop me from reaching my dream of becoming a primary school teacher.

However, thanks to the ongoing support from family, friends and the University I overcame the immediate shock and was able to recognise that nothing had changed. I was still the same person, my difficulties had just been given a name. This diagnosis opened doors to a wide range of support, including extra time in assessments, computerised software (supporting reading, information processing and organisation) and scheduled one-to-one sessions with a specialist trained to support me with the academics at the University. Although it was clear that university was going to be difficult, I am not one to shy away from a challenge; I had worked hard to get to the level I was at, and I certainly wasn't going to give up.

I am becoming more comfortable in discussing my dyslexia with others, recognising that there are some people who see it as a disadvantage, especially in pursuing my career in teaching. However, I recognise that I am more equipped than others to identify and support pupils who are finding learning difficult, who are regularly upset and who feel they are never going to understand something. I am determined to become a teacher. Although at times I am frustrated by my dyslexia, I know that it has made me the dedicated, motivated person I am today and I would never change that.

What are the indicators and how are pupils assessed for dyslexia?

Early identification is crucial, and to be able to do this you need to be aware of the indicators. In the early years you need to identify at-risk indicators and strengths of individual pupils. Dyslexia is an accumulation of several areas of difficulties.

Some signs which may indicate dyslexia in young children

- Inability to crawl.
- Difficulty learning nursery rhymes.
- Inability to recognise rhyming words.
- May have had early signs of language difficulties and pronunciation of sounds.
- Muddles words and sounds, for example 'tar' for 'car' and 'beddie tear' instead of 'teddy bear'.
- Shows no interest in letters and words but enjoys being read to.
- Difficulties in sequencing, for example, dressing, colour sequences, instructions and alphabet recall.

(For examples of checklists for use in the early years, visit the online extras at: www.sagepub.co.uk/martindenham.)

The indicators for dyslexia in older children

One of the indicators in older children could be continuous reversal of letters, for example 'b' and 'd'. This alone does not mean the child is dyslexic, you need to observe what other areas of difficulty the pupil is experiencing.

Some difficulties which could indicate dyslexia in older children

- Confusion with directional language.
- Gross and fine motor skill difficulties.
- Continued difficulty in learning to read, write, spell and recall times tables.

(Continued)

(Continued)

- Poor concentration and appearing to be lacking in motivation.
- Frustration and anxiety and a lack of confidence in reading, writing, spelling and possibly mental mathematics.
- Disorganisation and forgetfulness; for example, following a timetable, remembering homework and equipment for particular lessons.
- Length of time to complete a task or respond to questions due to a difficulty in processing and retaining instructions.
- Adopting strategies such as inappropriate behaviour to avoid certain aspects of lessons which they find extremely challenging.

How are pupils assessed for dyslexia?

Initially, pupils are usually identified as having a difficulty with their language processing/literacy. It is worth enquiring with parents/carers or pre-school staff whether children have previously been referred to a SLT in their early years. The indicators are a good guide to form preliminary evidence that a pupil may be dyslexic. Teacher observational assessment is the best form of evidence; however, sometimes this needs to be substantiated with more formal diagnostic and standardised assessments. There are many assessments available to teachers and as dyslexia is a combination of many factors one assessment is never enough. All schools should possess a range of assessments that should be administered by qualified teachers. If you are to administer an assessment it is crucial to familiarise yourself with the manual and follow it precisely. Your SENCO should be able to tell you what is available. It is essential that you discuss your concerns with the parents/carers, preferably with the aid of your SENCO, and obtain their consent before you administer any formal assessment. These assessments will inform you of the interventions needed for the pupil and will provide good information if it is then necessary to proceed to a formal diagnosis, if requested. The tests listed in Table 10.1 should assist in the identification, screening or diagnosis of dyslexia.

Scotopic sensitivity or Irlen Syndrome

Some pupils are diagnosed with scotopic sensitivity or Irlen Syndrome (visual stress). This is a visual perception difficulty in which pupils are unable to recognise print in its usual format. The text may appear in swirls, blurry or seem to move and the pupil may not be able to see

Table 10.1 Useful Screening Tests for SpLD

Title	Publisher
P.R.E.S.T (Pre School Screening Test)	Pearsons Assessment
P.I.P.A (Pre-school and Primary Inventory of Phonological Awareness)	Pearsons Assessment
D.E.S.T (dyslexia Early Screening Test)	Pearsons Assessment
D.S.T (Junior) & (Secondary) (Dyslexia Screening Test)	Pearsons Assessment
BPVS (British Picture Vocabulary Scale)	GL Assessment
WRIT (Wide Range Intelligence Test)	
Kirklees Reading Test	(revised, Dyslexia Institute website, 1996)
Sentence Completion Test (free)	(Dyslexia Institute)
LIST – The Listening Skills Test	Pearsons Assessment
PhAB (Phonological Assessment Battery)	NFER Nelson (GL Assessment)
P.A.T – Phonological Abilities Test	Pearsons Assessment
Dyscalculia Screener	NFER Nelson (GL Assessment)
Dyslexia Screener	NFER Nelson (GL Assessment)
Quest	NFER Nelson
Wordchains	NFER Nelson (GL Assessment)
Listening Comprehension	NFER Nelson (GL Assessment)
W.R.A.T 4	B.D.A
Aston Index	L.D.A
Pre-literacy Skills Screen	Senter (AMS Educational)
Early Literacy Skills Screen	Senter (AMS Educational)
WRaPS (Word reading & Phonic Skills)	Hodder & Stoughton
Lucid CoPS (4–8 yrs)	Lucid Research Ltd
LASS (11–15 yrs)	Lucid Research Ltd
WIAT-11 UK for Teachers	Pearsons Assessment

Note: This is not an exhaustive list of assessments. None of the above in isolation will confirm that a pupil is dyslexic, but they can provide very good evidence.

spaces between words. This can sometimes be mistakenly diagnosed as dyslexia. However, scotopic sensitivity can sometimes co-exist with SpLD such as dyslexia. Providing pupils with coloured overlays or glasses with tinted lenses usually alleviates this difficulty. An assessment for this is usually carried out by an optometrist.

Indicators of visual stress

During observation the pupil may:

- have difficulty when looking at written pages;
- complain of headaches or feeling sick when reading;
- regularly turn away from written pages or be unable to look at them for fixed periods of time;
- move closer to or further away from the text when reading;
- rub their eyes;
- complain of eyes feeling itchy, tired and scratchy;
- comment that the words appear to move;
- be affected by different levels of light or glare off black print on white paper.

Strategies for supporting pupils with visual stress

- Change the background colour of the computer screen to meet individual preferences.
- Provide a choice of coloured papers to use for worksheets and other tasks.
- Change the interactive whiteboard background to a tinted colour (green and blue seem to be the most accepted colours).
- Provide different coloured markers so pupils can choose their preferred colour for writing on the whiteboard.
- Provide transparent colour reading rulers or coloured transparencies to place over reading materials.
- Use tinted mini whiteboards and flashcards.
- Check whether your school has any reading books with coloured pages, for example published by Barrington Stoke.

It is worth enquiring with your SENCO whether the school has a visual stress assessment pack.

Making your classroom dyslexia friendly

If pupils have severe dyslexia and/or have not been identified in the early stages of education they are likely to require individualised pro-grammes on a one-to-one or small group basis. This teaching can be led by a member of support staff under the supervision and direction of the class teacher. It is vital that these specific learning programmes are followed correctly and that time is given for learning and rein-forcement. Useful programmes in book form for those with moderate to severe dyslexia include:

- *The Hickey Multi-sensory Language Course* (Combley, 2000)
- *Sound Linkage: An Integrated Programme for Overcoming Reading Difficulties* (Hatcher et al., 2014)
- *Teaching Literacy to Learners with Dyslexia: A Multi-sensory Approach* (Kelly and Phillips, 2011)

You need to be mindful of the indicators in order to provide an inclusive learning experience for your pupils. Some strategies would include tell-ing the pupils the purpose of reading/writing the text before beginning and the time they have to complete the task (a timer may be useful for this). If you are asking them to write a story, choose what your focus is (e.g. the spelling, sentence structure or content) and share this with the pupil. Another way of providing an inclusive classroom is to use colour coding to support the pupil during their time in school.

Colour coding

- The teacher/pupil highlights key words (use acetate over text to protect if using a book).
- Regular use of coloured highlighter pens can be beneficial (preferably allow the pupil to select the colour). Examples of how this might be used are: a different colour for adjectives/nouns/verbs/specific sounds such as 'the boy went in the hot bath'.
- For those pupils who do not understand sentence structure colour coding can be used to highlight the capital letter and the full stop. As pupils learn more about sentence structure and punctuation colour coding can be used for speech marks, question marks, commas and colons.
- When proof reading the pupil can highlight words which he/she considers are incorrectly spelled. Please remember to limit the number of words you ask them to highlight to protect their self-esteem.
- When learning spellings pupils can choose to highlight the part of the word they know or the part they need to learn.
- Colour code key words for different subject areas, for example labelling all science equipment the same colour.
- Provide a colour coded timetable for different subjects.

Alternative methods of written recording

Teachers should provide a range of strategies for pupils to assist them in their planning of written information. This needs to take into account the pupils' learning preferences, strengths and styles. Some of the following strategies could be used:

- Lists
- Diagrams (using colour, pictures and symbols)
- Mind maps (using colour, pictures and symbols)
- Postit® Notes
- Audio and digital recordings
- Singing, rapping and music making
- iPads (notebooks) and computers

Within your day-to-day teaching you need to consider whether the pupil really needs to write the date, learning objective and success criteria in every lesson (what are they learning from this?). This takes time away from the actual learning.

Consider the following for your classroom:

- display an alphabet frieze at an accessible height regardless of Key Stage;
- have tactile letters and numbers (felt, magnetic and wooden) available;
- provide written information rather than asking them to copy from the board;
- label as many objects in the classroom as possible (on coloured paper);
- provide visual prompts such as mind maps, pictures and diagrams;
- provide key words on topics on individual tables, displays or in a notebook prior to what is being taught – this is essential;
- use a visual timetable to show the structure of the day;
- use simple fonts such as Calibri or Arial, minimum size 12 point;
- use dictaphones to allow playback of important information and instructions;
- use voice activated technology if available for older pupils;
- use mnemonics to help letter recall and spelling – simultaneous oral spelling and cued spelling are spelling systems which can be adopted – also use electronic spell checkers and phonic dictionaries such as ace dictionaries alongside personalised dictionaries (as in telephone directory with A–Z tabs);
- use ongoing prompts (where, when, why, who and what) in all subjects to ensure that pupils have addressed all aspects of written work;

- create a quiet work area if possible;
- provide ear defenders;
- provide raised writing blocks.

The particular needs of pupils with dyspraxia

The word dyspraxia comes from 'dys', meaning difficulty, and 'praxis', indicating the ability to use the body as a skilled tool. Dyspraxia is usually described as a developmental dyspraxia, motor learning difficulty, developmental co-ordination disorder or percepto-motor dysfunction. This tells us that dyspraxia is difficulty with movement and co-ordination and carrying out tasks. It has a detrimental impact on both fine motor skills (such as picking up a small object and handwriting) and gross motor skills (running, jumping and hopping), and in some cases it can affect speech. The exact causes are still unknown; dyspraxia is believed to be due to a disruption in the way messages from the brain are transmitted to the body. It is believed that dyspraxia affects one child in every 30, with a ratio of 4/5:1 boys to girls (Dyspraxia Foundation, 2014).

Common signs of dyspraxia

- Not achieving expected developmental milestones, particularly in sitting, standing, crawling, walking and talking, in comparison to other children of the same age.
- Has difficulty dressing and undressing.
- Poor short-term memory.
- Falls over frequently and has difficulty with stairs.
- Unable to hop, jump, skip, run, dance and kick a ball.
- Difficulties following and remembering instructions.
- Dyspraxia can impact on eye movement and therefore impacts on the ability to read.

How to support a pupil with dyspraxia in school

Once you find out that a pupil in your class has dyspraxia you will need to plan how you are going to support them. Below are some suggestions you may find useful.

Ways to provide support for pupils with dyspraxia

- Provide a plan of the school to support them in navigating the school premises.
- Advise parents to purchase clothes without buttons or laces as this can cause unnecessary anxiety when they have to dress/undress in a given time.
- For handwriting exercises use multi-sensory approaches to letter formation, in sand, air writing, scribing on the pupil's back, stencilling and pencil/pen grips.
- Practise gross and fine motor skills through wobble boards, pegging items onto a washing line, throwing and catching a range of objects in different sizes such as balloons, tennis balls, large foam balls and bean bags.
- Don't overfill cups as the drink will be likely to spill.
- Encourage the playing of sports to develop co-ordination skills and confidence.

 Reflective activity

Jack is nine years old and is in mainstream school. He has recently been diagnosed with dyspraxia. He is often chosen last in Physical Education sessions. What can you do to support him? (A Suggestion is given at the end of the chapter.)

The particular needs of pupils with dyscalculia

The word dyscalculia comes from 'dys', meaning difficulty, and 'calculia', from calculate. Pupils with dyscalculia have a specific difficulty with mathematics and often are unable to acquire the basic concepts that underpin the skills necessary for performing mathematical procedures. This can impact on very simple activities, such as counting and comparing small numbers (e.g. Which is bigger, 2 or 4?) (Hannell, 2005). They may be unable to visualise numbers or see relationships between numbers. Other difficulties are counting groups of numbers, recalling times tables or facts and using strategies for basic calculations. Pupils with dyscalculia will often have difficulties with working memory, so during timed assessments they are likely to become particularly stressed.

Common signs of dyscalculia

- Slower responses to number problems than pupils of the same age.
- Failing to understand the basic concepts of number.
- Counting on fingers and an inability to recognise small numbers without counting.
- Difficulty in counting dots in array.
- Difficulty in visualising.
- Inability to tell the time from an analogue clock.
- Forgetting previously understood procedures quickly.
- Being poor at estimation tasks, will often count one by one in a counting tasks.
- Difficulty with estimating time (the numerical side), knowing what time to leave to get to school on time.
- Avoidance of tasks and games which involve calculations.

How to support a pupil with dyscalculia in school

- Ensure that they have a good view of the board and that distractions are minimised, such as noises from other classrooms or outside.
- Recap prior learning as it is likely they will have short-term memory difficulties.
- Target their areas of weakness, focus on multi-sensory learning approaches.
- Have a variety of choices of pencil sizes and grips.
- Use a visual timetable to show the structure of the day.
- Remind them of tasks part way through a lesson.
- Support pupils during tests and assessments, allowing additional time for working out.
- Don't ask them to solve mathematical problems in front of the rest of the class.
- Praise all achievements and look for signs of anxiety.

CASE STUDY

Supporting a pupil with working memory difficulties

Emily, aged 10 years, was always forgetting what she needed for school as she could not remember what was needed each day, or which day it was. A system

(Continued)

(Continued)

was needed to develop her independence and to support her in recalling what she needed for school. The parents and class teacher decided to create 'days of the week reminders' for school and home to assist her in remembering everything she needed. It was hoped that this would resolve the issue of her not having what she needed in school when she needed it. The family were also concerned that if she did not have strategies to remember everything she needed in primary school, she would become very distressed in secondary school when pupils move classrooms and get detention if they are not prepared and organised. The family purchased a clock which displayed the day, month and date, and wrote the following routine on a chalk board in the kitchen; a laminated version was also in her school bag and was displayed in the classroom:

Monday: dinner money, PE bag, house keys

Tuesday: return homework, swimming kit, house keys

Wednesday: reading book, trainers and house keys

Thursday: spelling test practice sheet, house keys

Friday: weekend bag for sleepover and collect homework

Saturday: complete homework

Sunday: get bag ready for Monday

The strategy worked well and Emily's confidence improved. However, if the system is not used she will return to forgetting what is needed day to day.

As with any area of exceptionality it is what you do with the information that will support the pupil. If you discover through screening that a pupil has a specific learning difficulty, you need then to provide focussed interventions. Through screening you will be able to identity the pupil's strengths and weaknesses on which you can build.

Additional resources

As well as the resources you'll find at **www.sagepub.co.uk/martindenham** you should also take a look at the following:

Advanced Training Materials Online Resource, www.advanced-training. org.uk: This website has a range of modules you can access for free including: Autism, Moderate Learning Difficulties, Behaviour, Emotional and Social Difficulties, SpLD and Speech, Language and Communication Needs.

Emerson, J. (2013) *The Dyscalculia Assessment*. London: Bloomsbury Educational. This assessment tool allows you to pinpoint difficulties and then produce a personalised learning plan to support a pupil's particular area of need.

Hannell, G. (2005) *Dyscalculia: action plans for successful learning in mathematics*. London: David Fulton Publishers.

Inclusion Development Programme (IDP) Online Resource, www.idponline.org.uk: An extremely useful resource which aims to improve outcomes for all pupils and to narrow gaps through early recognition. You can self-assess your knowledge in teaching pupils with dyslexia.

International Dyslexia Association, http://eida.org/: This website includes a range of free resources and factsheets to support you in teaching children and young people with a range of specific learning difficulties.

Kelly and Phillips have produced two books which will support you in teaching pupils with dyslexia: *Teaching Literacy to Learners with Dyslexia: A Multi-sensory Approach*, and (together with Symes) *Assessment of Learners with Dyslexic Type Difficulties*. Both are published by SAGE.

Rogers, J. and Bourne, L. (2001) *Achieving Dyslexia Friendly Schools: Resource Pack*. London: British Dyslexia Association. This resource is available to download free from the British Dyslexia Association website. There is sound advice and guidance on how to create a dyslexia friendly learning environment.

The British Dyslexia Association, http://www.bdadyslexia.org.uk/: This website includes a range of free downloadable resources. The information and activities tab is particularly useful.

The Dyspraxia Foundation, www.dyspraxiafoundation.org.uk/: A website with extensive advice and guidance. There is a professionals' section where you can gain access to a range of journals and other publications.

Possible solutions

For the Reflective activity on p. 120

You need to have a system which means that pupils who are less skilled in PE are not chosen last. The most logical solution is for you to select the teams in a fair and manageable way. Say, for example, you need two teams: give each child a number or coloured sticker which will represent the group they are in.

CHAPTER 11

SEVERE, PROFOUND AND MULTIPLE LEARNING DIFFICULTIES

Jan Patterson and Chris Roberts

Key ideas explored in this chapter

- What do we mean by SLD and PMLD?
- What are some of the causes of SLD and PMLD?
- How to create a purposeful learning environment to meet the needs of pupils with SLD and PMLD
- Effective teaching approaches for pupils with PMLD

What do we mean by SLD and PMLD?

Pupils with SLD have significant intellectual or cognitive impairments. There are an increasing number of pupils with SLD attending mainstream schools as well as specialist contexts. These pupils need support with all aspects of school life and will generally be working below level 1 of the National Curriculum. They are often described as having global developmental delay (GDD), which means they have not reached two or more developmental milestones.

Pupils with SLD are generally achieving between performance levels P4 to P8. The P levels/scales were developed by the Department for Education and Employment in 1998 to support the target setting process for pupils with SEN working within level 1 and range from P1 at the very early stages of intellectual development to P8 which is just below level 1 of the NC. You can still access the revised guidance *Supporting the Target Setting Process* (DfEE, 2001) at www.gov.uk.

Pupils with PMLD have complex learning needs. They have very severe learning difficulties with other significant difficulties such as physical disabilities, sensory impairments or severe medical conditions. They are generally functioning at the very early stages of development and achieving between levels P1 to P3/4. These pupils need a sensory based curriculum which is broken down into very small steps.

A term often used is 'complex and additional needs'. This rather broad term covers pupils with cognitive and learning difficulties together with one, some or all of the following: behavioural, emotional and social difficulties; autistic spectrum disorders; speech, language and communication needs; hearing impairment; visual impairment; and medical and physical disabilities. Clearly, pupils with PMLD will come under this heading.

What are some of the causes of SLD and PMLD?

There are several causes of SLD and PMLD. These are:

- chromosomal and genetic conditions, such as Down syndrome and Fragile X syndrome;
- infections such as congenital rubella, or other intrauterine factors;
- injury or physical trauma, such as road traffic SEN accidents;
- toxins, such as alcohol and certain medications;
- medical conditions that restrict development.

 Key points to remember

- Whatever the causes or reasons for the pupils' learning difficulties, they are all pupils with additional needs, they are not their disabilities.
- It is vital that you listen and observe and give each pupil their 'voice', enabling them be an active partner in the learning process.
- It is your responsibility to find out about the pupil's specific needs. Speak to the SENCO and other members of the team to learn as much as you can.

How to create a purposeful learning environment to meet the needs of pupils with SLD and PMLD

In order to meet the educational needs of pupils with SLD and PMLD it is essential to plan and create a learning environment which will best suit the pupils within the particular group. Their needs may vary greatly; however, there are some key approaches and strategies which will be useful for you to consider as they have been used successfully over many years by practitioners in a range of specialist settings with pupils across all age ranges.

Above all, this is a learning environment; it should be stimulating, to encourage pupils to access equipment and participate in activities. Many pupils with SLD are not motivated to learn in the same way as typically developing pupils, so it is important for the adults working with them to observe closely and find out what interests and excites the pupils to inform planning for learning.

As pupils with SLD and PMLD are functioning at the early stages of development it is useful to consider best practice from the EYFS (DfE, 2014b). When planning your learning environment and teaching approaches, adapt this practice to make it appropriate to the age and interests of your pupils. For example, areas of the room designated for certain activities help pupils' understanding and awareness. It gives an explicit structure for those pupils whose level of understanding means they cannot yet anticipate what will happen next. Pupils who are achieving at the early stages of development benefit from multi-sensory approaches to the curriculum. This means incorporating using as many of the senses as possible in activities. These approaches are also useful for pupils who have sensory impairments, as they can use more than one of their other senses to access the activity. Sensory stories, which are discussed later in this chapter, are great for doing this.

There are a range of therapies used in some special educational provisions which complement and/or extend activities in classrooms. These include:

- **Hydrotherapy:** carried out in a hydrotherapy pool. Some schools may take pupils to a local pool. Working with pupils in warm water gives them a sensory experience and provides an opportunity for close contact and trust building. The pool also provides opportunities for physiotherapy.
- **Physiotherapy:** many pupils will have physiotherapy needs. Schools may have their own physiotherapists, or more likely regular visits from

NHS staff. It is common practice for class teachers and support staff to learn some simple routines to carry out with their pupils.

- **Rebound therapy:** gentle bouncing with pupils on a trampoline. It provides a very powerful sensory experience, which many pupils love. There is a real opportunity here, as with the other therapies, to observe pupils' communication. If the pupil is enjoying the activity and we stop, what happens? Start again. Was there a cue from the pupil? It may be that the pupil 'asks' for the bouncing to start.
- **Light therapy:** often used in a light/sensory studio to develop an understanding of cause and effect by accessing bubble tubes, fibre optics, and colour projected images using a switch.
- **Sound therapy:** music, visual effects and resonance board accessed by breaking a sound beam. The beam can be broken by any movement made by the pupil, including blinking their eyes.
- **Music therapy:** in its purest form this would be a one-to-one therapy. The music therapist follows the pupils' interests using different forms of musical instruments, sounds and voice.

Staff within specialist contexts often undertake additional training in one or more of these therapies and work with individuals or small groups of pupils in designated areas or rooms. It is important, as the teacher, to understand these therapies and their place within the whole curriculum offered to each individual pupil, so that you can incorporate them in your planning with the help of the trained staff member who delivers the therapy.

Activity suggestion

The use of multi-sensory cues for days of the week

Each day of the week is allocated a visual, auditory, tactile, olfactory (smell) and gustatory (taste) cue. These can be used as the introduction for the pupils to begin and review each day. These multi-sensory cues used over time give pupils a range of cues they can link to the days of the week, not just a name, which may be meaningless to them.

Monday: red lights and voiles are used, classical music is played, smooth texture, warming aroma and apple to taste.

(Continued)

(Continued)

Tuesday: blue lights and voiles, 'blues' music, rough texture, bergamot aroma and pear to taste.

Wednesday: yellow lights and voiles, mellow music, furry texture, lemon aroma and lemon to taste.

Thursday: green lights and voiles, country music, sticky texture, eucalyptus aroma and lime to taste.

Friday: white lights and voiles, jazz music, cotton wool texture, cypress aroma and milk to taste.

Visual timetables with 'objects of reference'

Visual timetables or schedules are used widely in specialist provision. They are used as part of a multi-sensory approach with the use of symbols and signing. They support pupils in many ways, providing a visual structure for part or all their day or for individual tasks. They are often used with pupils who have autism, difficulty understanding language, those who are anxious or have behavioural difficulties. Many pupils are visual learners, so visual timetables build on their strengths. The timetable may be made up of photographs, pictures or symbols ordered from left to right. The photo/picture/symbol can be accompanied by an 'object of reference'. This is an object that has been chosen to represent an activity or event and gives a clue about what is about to happen. It is also useful to incorporate the use of a 'now' and 'next' board, as most pupils with SLD have a level of understanding in the 'here and now'.

Effective teaching approaches for pupils with PMLD

This section is intended to give an insight into some of the techniques and strategies that are commonly seen in operation in a classroom environment for pupils with PMLD.

Intensive interaction

Intensive interaction is a commonly used tool in the classroom for pupils with PMLD (and is very successfully with pupils with autism). The purpose of intensive interaction is to create an enjoyable and understandable social experience for the pupil. Its essence is to find a way of responding to the pupil's behaviour which attracts their attention and promotes enjoyment and interaction. In the classroom setting what will be seen is a member of staff sitting with an individual pupil. The staff member may be copying an action or mimicking the sound that the pupil makes. The intention is that the pupil will respond with the same action or sound with the intention of provoking a response. The member of staff and pupil are starting to communicate. The skill is in how well they observe, copy and interpret the actions of the pupil.

Intensive interaction is important as it teaches the pupil how to enjoy being with another person and to develop the ability to attend to that person; it also teaches and promotes the development of concentration and attention span. This is achieved through sharing personal space, eye contact, facial expression, simple vocalisation, and giving and receiving tactile stimuli. As with many of the strategies used with pupils with PMLD, this is something that can be seen happening naturally between mother and baby.

CASE STUDY

Intensive interaction

Joe, aged 18, would sit in his chair rocking his head backwards and forwards quite violently. As he was doing this he would vocalise 'ha-he'. I sat opposite him and started repeating 'ha-he' after him. After a little while he stopped rocking and concentrated on the vocalising, starting to smile when I repeated what he had said. After a few sessions (5–10 minutes in length) he would make his sound followed by eye contact, inviting me to say 'ha-he' in reply; this repeated several times. This then developed by me holding out a hand, Joe placed his hand in mine. This started a game where I would withdraw my hand and he would put out his hand, my hand would go onto his, which he would then withdraw, and so on. All the time the eye contact and the 'ha-he' was happening. Joe clearly enjoyed this interaction because he would smile throughout the session, and if I stopped he would try to initiate it over again by rocking his head backwards and forwards. If I re-engaged, this behaviour would stop. I found that I could end our 'communication' without the negative response by saying and signing 'bye' or 'finish'.

Tacpac®

On their website Tacpac® describes itself as follows: 'Tacpac® is a revolutionary activity pack that combines touch and music to promote communication and social interaction, sensory, neurological and emotional development.' It is simple to perform and a very effective activity for pupils with PMLD and lower functioning pupils working at P4/P5. Tacpac® has also been successfully used with adult learners who are mobile and higher functioning, pupils with autism, people with global developmental delay, tactile defensiveness and sensory impairments.

The essence of Tacpac® is to combine music, specifically composed, with a tactile stimulus, which is usually applied using an easily obtainable object. For example, flicking with a washing-up mop is used in one of the sets. Success depends on aligning the basic beat of the music with the touch of the object on the body. The music should never be altered, as the pupil will rely on the variety of melody, harmony, texture, tempo and timbre for their sensory reference. All this has been carefully woven into the specifically composed music. The session is carried out in a quiet environment and usually on a one-to-one ratio. Tacpac® should never be delivered in a room where there are any other sensory stimuli (e.g. a sensory room). Consistency is important for the pupils' anticipation, predictability and relaxation. The practitioner is able to form a relationship with the pupil, and hopefully observe pleasure and anticipation in the pupil; this communication bond between pupil and practitioner may then develop over subsequent sessions.

CASE STUDY

Tacpac®

Gemma is a 14-year-old pupil with autism and very SLD. She exhibited very challenging and sometimes violent behaviour and was very reluctant to interact with other staff or pupils.

I wanted to develop a relationship with her so decided to try Tacpac®. I timetabled three sessions a week (each session taking around 30 minutes – you may take up to an hour) and made a start in the first half of the autumn term; another pupil in the class was also joining in with the session with a TA in a quiet corner of the class. Initially sessions were very short-lived; the music would start, I would sit down and my pupil would stand and walk away. Slowly, over a few weeks, she sat for longer periods and started to allow me to use the tactile stimuli. After a few months she was showing a preference for particular stimuli and showing clear anticipation, prompted by the music and the presentation of the object used for the stimulus. Around this time she was also preparing herself for her Tacpac® session; she would go to the cupboard and collect the Tacpac® pack, she would also allow me to take off her jumper (it is better to apply the tactile stimulus to bare arms), which in itself was a major step as previously any attempt to take off a jumper would be met with hostility. She would then sit ready to start. I would then position my own chair directly in front of hers.

During the winter/spring term she was making increased eye contact and was clearly enjoying the whole Tacpac® process. The last part of a Tacpac® session is the relaxation phase. I would signal the start of this by moving my chair next to hers, something that she liked and responded positively to. I introduced a blanket to this phase and swaddled her; she responded by completely relaxing and laying her head on my shoulder. This build-up of trust took until Easter. I continued with regular sessions throughout the summer term with the same positive response. I would be lying if I was to say it was all plain sailing, it was not. Even when we had reached the point of trust there were occasional days when she was not in the mood (perhaps not feeling well or had been upset on the way to school) and walked away.

Sensory stories

Everyone enjoys good stories. Great pleasure is derived from listening to a familiar story over and over again. We know what is going to happen and we wait with anticipation. For our pupils with PMLD this still applies but in a different way. It is unlikely that the story will be understood and in many cases they will not be able to see the pictures as many people with PMLD also have visual impairment to varying degrees. The pleasure comes in the way the story is told.

The telling of 'sensory stories' is widely used with pupils with PMLD and probably to a lesser degree pupils with SLD. Stories are chosen that will catch and hold the attention of pupils who are at a very early stage in language development. As each page of the story is told pupils are given a sensory cue, which could be visual, tactile, olfactory (sense of smell), auditory or a combination. For example, in a section of the story it's raining, so water is flicked at the pupils; in another story there is a fire, so a smoky aromatic is passed round for each pupil to smell.

The same story is told many times over a period of time so that pupils get to know and enjoy the sequence. Over time they may start to anticipate the different stimuli; this could be in a very positive way, but could equally be a negative response if there is a section that they know they do not like.

There are many commercially produced sensory stories on the market. The better ones come with clear notes and background to the theory behind the concept. Try using commercially produced stories for some sessions and your own adapted stories for others. Take a story that has an easy sequence and then perhaps condense it, then link a sensory cue to each page. With these adapted stories try to make the 'telling' a performance which engages the pupils and promotes as much response as possible. To do this well you need to be enthusiastic and animated.

It is important that observations are made of the pupil's reactions and that these are recorded on record sheets during the story. It is useful for a member of staff to sometimes record the responses of pupils with a video camera for later review, as it is difficult to combine the role of story teller and assessor.

 Key points to remember

- Video records are great for reviewing pupils' reactions, so have the equipment ready for use at all times.
- Make the story an occasion, something special every time you tell it!
- Be animated when telling the story – if you are enjoying it the pupils will too.

 Reflective activity

You go into a classroom where the pupils are being read a familiar story. You are told that the pupils like the story and always seem to be engaged when it is read. How could you develop it into a sensory story?

Think of a story you know well, break it down into up to 12 parts and see if you can assign a sensory cue to those parts.

When preparing a sensory story it is worth reading the story to the pupils, or observing the pupils as it is being read by the familiar adult. Note the parts of the story where the pupils are particularly engaged, and whether or not there is a specific cue that could be linked to some sensory input. Go for obvious cues for sensory input, ones that will be readily anticipated by the pupils. For instance, if water comes into the story, that could be the cue to flick water at the pupils, or to allow them to put their hands into a bowl of water.

From experience, it is usually best to select a story that has a very definite sequence of events. Each event should be considered as a cue for a sensory input. Your sensory input should relate to some aspect of the event that can be exaggerated when telling the story. *Going on a Bear Hunt* would be a really good story to start with; there is a very clear sequence of events and each can easily be allocated a relatively obvious sensory cue.

CASE STUDY

Sensory stories

Ahmed, aged 17, has a great sense of humour and really enjoys sensory stories. In one of our stories he particularly likes the 'it was raining' part. On hearing the phrase he starts to smile and looks towards the 'reader'. The sensory cue linked to 'it was raining' is for the reader or assistant to flick water at the pupils in turn. When it comes to his turn and he is flicked with water he always has a great big grin on his face. He also knows that if he looks at his TA she will also get water flicked at her; he thinks this is great and rocks in his chair with an even bigger smile. In this example Ahmed has learnt to recognise a key phrase. He anticipates the stimulus, which he enjoys. He has also learnt to control who else receives the stimulus by communicating with the reader using a look (gaze).

 Key points to remember

- Commercially produced sensory stories are usually very good. Making your own resources can be very time consuming. For the trainee teacher, picking a sensory story from the shelf (if available) would probably be the best starting point.
- Once you know your pupils and understand better the principles of sensory stories, then it is very rewarding to create your own.
- Be guided by the reactions of the pupils and the staff you are working with.

Eye gaze

For most of us eye contact is a very important part of communication. For pupils with PMLD who have no verbal means of communication, particularly if this is combined with cerebral palsy, eye gaze may be their only means of communication (we must remember that for many of our pupils with PMLD some degree of visual impairment may also be present).

The communication partner (practitioner/parent/carer) needs to position themselves in such a way that they are at the pupil's eye level and can make eye contact. At its most basic level, just making eye contact is a start of the communication process. If the pupil is able to look at an object and then back at the partner then communication has started, this has signalled an interest in something. This basic communication strategy is seen to work very effectively with babies getting the attention of their mothers.

Once it has been established that eye contact can be made it may now be possible to use objects, simple symbols or pictures to help pupils make simple choices. In the first instance holding an object in each hand in front of the pupil and asking 'Which one?', for example. Watch where the pupil's gaze goes and ask a confirmation question 'This one?'. This process is repeated until the pupil knows that they are able to make a choice. The progression from this is to start using simple pictures or symbols. It may be that the choice being made is yes or no, rather than a choice between two objects.

Clearly for eye gaze to work there must be a one-to-one ratio between pupil and partner. In some cases it may also be useful to have a 'checker' sitting behind the communication partner to confirm the direction of eye gaze. Eye gaze communication will be discussed further later on in the chapter.

The use of switches

Switches are commonly used in the classroom for pupils with PMLD. They are used to help the pupil relate cause and effect. Figure 11.1 shows examples of two different switches.

The switches are connected to an object that shows a very definite effect. This could be a toy, a light, a sound, a computer screen/whiteboard, any obvious change in the environment for the pupil. There are many switches on the market, which are typically big, robust and often brightly coloured. Pupils will access their switches in different ways depending on their own specific need. Usually a switch will be operated by pressing with the hand; pupils with Cerebral Palsy may have so little control of their arms that they use a mouth switch or a head switch. The switch will be linked to its output object either directly, by wire or wirelessly.

At its most basic, pressing the switch once will cause an immediate effect; a more complex system is that an increasing number of presses are required to either build up to or cause the effect. There are a number

Figure 11.1 Example of switches used for pupils with PMLD

of examples of these type of switches on the market. Freely available is the SEN Switcher (www.northerngrid.org/resource/sen-switcher) program, which can be used with pupils using an interactive whiteboard. Whatever the complexity of the system it is vital that the pupil can detect a direct link between pressing the switch (cause) and the result of pressing the switch (effect). The effect must be a motivator for the pupil, for example, something that they enjoy. To get an idea of what is available you can look at a selection of special needs resources catalogues (e.g. *Inclusive Technology*). Many of the catalogues also include useful information on how to use switches effectively in the classroom.

CASE STUDY

Using switches

Amy loves to sit on a vibrating mat draped across a comfy chair. The mat is connected to a control box (switches) that has a number of buttons, each controlling some aspect of the vibration delivered by the mat. She is given the control box and loves to press the buttons. She learnt which button generates the highest level vibration. She also likes to get involved in a game where we

(Continued)

(Continued)

turn the unit off, she will turn it back on! She makes it very clear that she is enjoying the experience with her smiles and laughter.

In the classroom for pupils with PMLD many examples will be observed of pupils getting great pleasure controlling some aspect of their environment by operating simple switches; they are learning basic cause and effect.

The importance of sensory play

Sensory play is an essential activity common in all classrooms for pupils with PMLD. Pupils will be engaged in 'play' activities that stimulate their senses. This may be touching and manipulating sand or play dough, handling toys and objects with different tactile properties, playing with simple musical instruments to make sounds, looking into mirrors or watching lighting effects.

In many classrooms for pupils with PMLD you will find a sensory room. This will commonly have a light bubble tube. This is a clear tube (often 1–2 metres tall) filled with liquid, light is shone into this and bubbles are created in the liquid. There is often a switch that pupils can use to control the colours in the tube. There will probably be projectors and light colour washes, again often under the control of the pupils. A sound system can add to the room by introducing music or specific sound effects. An example of a sensory room is shown in Figure 11.2.

Another common resource is the ball pool; this is an enclosed area which is filled with plastic balls. Pupils are put into, or allowed to climb into the pool; weight is distributed differently and the effect is whole-body stimulation. Pupils will commonly show great pleasure when engaging in sensory play. The sensory room gives pupils the opportunity to relax and be immersed in controlled stimulation.

 Key points to remember

- In all of the activities described the practitioner is required to make careful observations. To look for responses from the pupils to identify likes and dislikes. Observations of responses should be recorded and used to inform future sessions.
- The practitioner is always part of the process and must take every opportunity to form a relationship with the pupil, to look for communication opportunities and to make every effort to develop these.

Figure 11.2 A sensory room showing lighting options

▦ **Reflective activity**

You have a placement with a group of pupils with PMLD you are asked to observe for the first week. How do you engage with the pupils in order to begin to plan for their learning in week 2? (Some suggestions are given at the end of the chapter.)

In this chapter the few teaching methods described require a high level of concentration from the practitioner and at times a high degree of emotional involvement. A day working in a classroom for pupils with PMLD often results in being physically and emotionally drained. Progress will be very slow. However, when those small steps are made, when there is that first interaction, the reward is HUGE.

Additional resources

As well as the resources you'll find at **www.sagepub.co.uk/martindenham** you should also take a look at the following:

Pete Wells, Portland Academy Sunderland has a wide range of free sensory stories, switch accessible activities, PowerPoint slides and guidance notes accessible on the school website: www. portlandcollege.org/curriculum/sensory-stories/. In the curriculum tab you will also find a range of other resources to use with pupils with a range of difficulties.

Phoebe Caldwell has uploaded some very good examples of intensive interaction on YouTube. There are a range of videos showing interactions with pupils across the age ranges with a range of needs. The videos show how you can use touch and body language to engage with pupils to develop communication and interaction.

Tacpac® and their training can be found at www.tacpac.co.uk. The website also includes links to research articles on the benefits of using Tacpac®. The Top Tips section also includes useful advice for delivering effective sessions.

The reader should go to the Internet and search www.youtube for clips on 'eye-gaze communication' and 'babies communicating'. Of particular interest, search for 'still face experiment'. You will see interesting clips of mothers and babies and social interactions.

Possible solutions

For the Reflective activity on p. 137

Observation, interaction and communication are crucial if you are to have success working with pupils with PMLD. During your first week observe the interactions that staff have with the pupils, what communication strategies are being used. Find out what motivates the pupils, and how they respond to the motivators. You will need to talk with staff to gain as much knowledge as you can about what makes the pupils 'tick'. Have a look through the current assessment levels for the pupils and find out whether any specific targets have been set. Although you have been asked to observe, ask whether you can join in with staff and pupils to allow yourself to become known by the pupil.

CHAPTER 12

OTHER AREAS OF EXCEPTIONALITY

Karen Horridge, Sarah Martin-Denham and Denise Murray

Key ideas explored in this chapter

- How to find reliable medical information
- Attention deficit hyperactivity disorders (ADHD)
- Cystic fibrosis
- Duchenne muscular dystrophy
- Epilepsies
- Type 1 diabetes

How to find reliable medical information

This chapter will include an overview of some types of difficulties a pupil may encounter such as genetic, neurological and environmental illnesses, syndromes and conditions. Each of these areas of exceptionality will have an outline with suggestions of how they can be supported in school. Due to the vast number of areas of need it would not be possible to outline them all, so links to useful sources will be provided at the end of the chapter.

There are between 4,000 and 6,000 diagnosed genetic disorders. It is estimated that one in 25 pupils is affected by a genetic disorder and therefore 30,000 babies and pupils are newly diagnosed in the UK each year. Some genetic disorders are apparent at birth while others are diagnosed at different ages and sometimes into adulthood (Genetic Disorders UK, 2014).

It is important to remember that there are many children who remain undiagnosed. SWAN UK (Syndromes Without A Name) is a project run by Genetic Alliance UK and offers support and information to families who have an undiagnosed genetic condition. These families face particular challenges as they are uncertain about what the future holds for their child. They will not know whether their child will ever walk, talk or what their life expectancy will be.

Attention deficit hyperactivity disorder (ADHD)

Attention deficit hyperactivity disorder (ADHD) is also known as attention deficit disorder (ADD) and hyperkinetic disorder. ADHD affects around 4 in 100 school-aged pupils in the UK and is believed to have both genetic and environmental links. It is the most common behavioural disorder in the UK, and is around three times more common in boys than in girls (Contact a Family, 2014). It is a fairly common condition that mainly affects a pupil's behaviour. There may also be concerns with the pupil's intellectual, social and psychological development as well as the ADHD.

The primary characteristics of ADD/ADHD are inattention and impulsivity, and with ADHD there is the addition of hyperactivity. The signs and symptoms a pupil with ADD has depend on which characteristics predominate.

Pupils with ADD/ADHD may be:

- inattentive, but not hyperactive or impulsive;
- hyperactive and impulsive, but able to pay attention;
- inattentive, hyperactive and impulsive (the most common form of ADD/ADHD).

Effective management of ADHD/ADD

To ensure the effective management of ADHD/ADD schools may need to provide:

- **A Behaviour Plan:** pupils with ADD/ADHD are capable of appropriate classroom behaviour, but they need structure and clear expectations. The behaviour plan should be developed with the parents/carers and the pupil. The plan will include specific goals (rules to follow) and daily positive reinforcement, as well as worthwhile rewards. It should also include corrective actions (what will happen if the rules are not adhered to).
- **A team who are consistent:** the behaviour plan needs to be followed routinely by every member of staff throughout the day.
- **A low-stimulus environment:** the pupil needs to be seated away from doors and windows, towards the front of the class-room where they can see who is teaching them. You will need to plan movement breaks into the lessons. Providing structure through lists, timetables (visual if necessary), deadlines and regular reminders (including timers) will encourage the pupils to stay on task.
- **A care plan:** to assess what care is needed and how it will be provided.
- **Trained staff to dispense medication:** some pupils are pre-scribed medication for ADHD/ADD, most commonly methylpheni-date, slow-release methylphenidate and atomoxetine.
- **A designated member of staff:** to liaise with parents.

 Reflective activity

It is your third week with your class and you are told you have a pupil starting tomorrow who has a diagnosis of ADHD. What information do you need to find out and who from?

Cystic fibrosis

Cystic fibrosis (CF) is an inherited chronic disease that affects the lungs and digestive system. The prevalence of CF is one in every 2,500 newborn babies. A faulty gene and its protein product cause the body to produce unusually thick, sticky mucus that:

- clogs the lungs and leads to lung infections that lead to lung dam-age which can be life-threatening;
- obstructs the pancreas and stops natural enzymes from helping the body break down and absorb food.

Effective management of cystic fibrosis

To ensure the effective management of cystic fibrosis schools may need to provide:

- **Physiotherapy:** to help clear mucus and reduce the risk of infection. Ensure that there are good links with the paediatric physiotherapist, with parental consent, who can provide direct training for staff.
- **Exercise plans:** to improve health in general and to reduce the use of medication.
- **Trained staff to dispense medication:** inhaled and intravenous drugs are taken to clear mucus and fight infections. Enzyme capsules are needed to help digest food. Diabetes can sometimes be a complicating factor.
- **Nutrition:** most pupils will eat three meals a day plus snacks to make sure that they have all the calories they need. The meals and snacks should have more calories and fat in them than other children as they have higher energy needs as they do not absorb their food as easily. It's also very important that they do not miss meals. A specialist diet may be needed if pupils have a school lunch. Ensure that there are good links with the paediatric dietician, with parental consent, who can provide advice and meal plans.
- **Infection control:** germs are carried by pupils who do *not* have CF which can be harmful to those with CF. Meticulous hand hygiene at all times is very important for the health and wellbeing of all pupils, especially when they have colds. Tissues should be used once only and thrown away in a waste bin with a lid that is emptied at least daily, or more often as required. Advice about adequate hand-washing techniques can be obtained from the school nurse or CF specialist nurse.
- **A designated member of staff:** to liaise with parents.

Every pupil with CF will have a CF nurse who will come into school to train staff and offer advice to ensure that the pupils stay as healthy as possible.

CASE STUDY

Working alongside health professionals

In preparation for a 14-year-old with CF joining the school, I attended his annual review meeting. This was important because I was able to meet and introduce myself to his parents and all the professionals involved with his care.

After talking to his CF specialist nurse I was able to arrange a date before he started for her to carry out a staff briefing and explain everything we would need to know to keep him safe and healthy. The nurse explained the importance of hygiene and did a tour of the school, pointing out what we needed to change before he started at the school. This included buying bins with lids for tissues to be disposed of and having a constant supply of soap in the toilets. We replaced bars of soap with soap dispensers because pupils kept taking the bars of soap home! We had to move some of our pets to a different area of the school as he is not allowed to handle them or clean them out. She also went through the medication he needed and how this was to be dispensed.

Although we have a designated member of staff for medication (she has undertaken an accredited medication training course run by the LA), everyone in the school, including lunch-time supervisors, was trained. This was to ensure that if he had anything to eat on visits or as a treat, even a sweet, all staff could calculate the number of enzyme capsules he would need. It was also important that all staff were aware of his inhaler and the need to use it before going outside to the playing field or forest school. The pupil also has a central venous access catheter, which is a tube that is inserted beneath his skin so that there is a simple, pain-free way for doctors or nurses to give him antibiotics or nutrients. It was vital that all staff were aware of this and knew what to do if it was damaged whilst the pupil was at school.

Once everyone had completed the training his parents were invited into school with him to produce a care plan. It was essential that the pupil was involved because it was his care plan. All the information needed was collated on the care plan including names and telephone numbers of his consultant, CF specialist nurse, General Practitioner, parents and emergency contact person. The care plan lists the name(s) of the medication he needs in school, the dosage, the time it needs to be taken and the name of the person who will dispense it. It also stated what to do in an emergency. Once it was completed it was signed by the parents and the designated person. Parents were given a copy and one was kept in school. While in school the parents met with the chef to develop a bespoke menu for their son which ensured that he had the foods that were necessary to keep him healthy. The medication he was given was recorded in his file with the date and time, the amount given, by whom, then it was signed by the member of staff.

School staff were frequently in touch with his parents either through the home-school diary, telephone calls or if the parents felt it was important to have a face-to-face meeting, through our open-door policy. If there was

(Continued)

(Continued)

something we were not sure about we would ask. He had the opportunity to take part in a weekly project working with glass at the Glass Centre. I did not know whether this was a safe environment for him, so before mentioning it to him I rang his mother who didn't know, so she rang the CF specialist nurse who said it would be perfectly all right for him to attend. By asking parents if we are not sure we are building trust, because they feel safe knowing that we will ask if in any doubt.

Unfortunately, the pupil was unwell with a chest infection for a term and needed intravenous antibiotics and steroids. He also developed diabetes. Before he came back to school after a short absence his care plan was updated to take into account his recent additional diagnosis. Parents met with our chef again and re-balanced his menu.

Four members of staff were trained to take his blood sugar readings and dispense insulin (although he could later self-administer with supervision). Again all staff were given diabetes training so that they would recognise hypoglycaemia/hyperglycaemia and know what to do about it.

The pupil has been in school for one year and two terms. He has made excellent progress academically and socially due to the excellent working relationships developed between school, parents and all the other professionals who work with him.

Duchenne muscular dystrophy

Duchenne muscular dystrophy is a genetic, degenerative condition which affects the muscles, causing muscle weakness, which usually only occurs in males. The muscle weakness is mainly in the 'proximal' muscles, which are those near the trunk of the body, around the hips and the shoulders, and is caused by an absence or reduction in the amount of dystrophin, a protein that helps keep muscle cells intact. This is all due to a faulty gene. As the condition progresses, muscle tissue experiences wasting and is eventually replaced by fat and fibrotic tissue. The prevalence is thought to be 1,000 boys with Duchenne muscular dystrophy born in the United Kingdom each year (Contact a Family, 2014).

Effective management of Duchenne muscular dystrophy

To ensure the effective management of Duchenne muscular dystrophy schools may need to provide:

- **Physiotherapy:** hydrotherapy (water exercises are concentric, which means muscle fibres are shortening so the stress on the muscles is reduced).
- **Access to a SLT:** speech and language problems may be associated, and muscle weakness may cause complications with feeding and swallowing.
- **Occupational therapists:** can offer practical support and equipment that may be needed, including wheelchairs, and can advise about adaptations to the school.
- **Trained staff to dispense medication:** including oral steroids, how to identify any side-effects such as osteoporosis (thinning of the bones), skin problems, mood and behavioural changes, and to monitor weight gain.
- **Trained staff to deliver intimate care:** staff to support pupils with toileting, which may include hoisting, moving and handling as well as changing incontinence pads.
- **A designated member of staff:** to liaise with parents.

 Reflective activity

Think of an activity you could do with a group of pupils to celebrate difference. Are there any useful picture books, film clips or poems that could be used to stimulate discussion of an aspect of diversity? (Some suggestions are given at the end of the chapter.)

Epilepsies

The epilepsies are conditions that affect the brain and usually involve recurrent, unprovoked seizures. Approximately 5 in every 100 people have an epileptic seizure at some time in their life. There are many different types of epilepsies and it is very important to have information specific to the individual pupil, with appropriate parental consent. During a seizure electrical activity in the brain changes, which causes a change in how the body behaves. Seizures vary from person to person, from appearing to be in a trance, to sudden jerks, to twisting postures, to losing consciousness and to having convulsions (shaking and jerking all over). The epilepsies in children are diagnosed by paediatricians with specific expertise in epilepsies. Epilepsies can wax and wane over time and can go away spontaneously. There are a range of treatments available, including anti-epileptic drugs (medications). It is important for those with epilepsies to have a healthy balanced diet and exercise, the same as everyone else (NHS, 2014).

Common seizure triggers are:

- missing dose(s) of medication;
- missing meals;
- being very tired or sleep-deprived;
- being unwell for any reason, e.g. having a cold;
- flickering or flashing lights or images, e.g. computer screen (photosensitive epilepsies).

What to do when a pupil has a seizure

Tonic-clonic seizures are when a person goes stiff, loses consciousness and may fall to the ground. This is then followed by jerking movements. It is likely at this point that they will have a blue tinge around their mouth due to irregular breathing. The jerking movements should subside within a minute or two. If this is the first time the pupil has had a seizure, a paramedic ambulance should be called immediately. If this is not the first seizure for this pupil, the pupil should have an individualised emergency health care plan or equivalent that should be followed and which will specify any emergency treatment to be given, including who to call. In any case, the pupil should be kept safe so that they cannot injure themselves on anything if their limbs are jerking. No attempt should be made to put fingers in the pupil's mouth as they are likely to bite, but a check should be made to ensure that they can breathe properly. Specialist training can be provided by the epilepsy nurse specialist or specialist community children's nurse and should be tailored to the individual pupil.

Type 1 diabetes

Type 1 diabetes is also known as 'insulin dependant' or 'juvenile diabetes'. This type of diabetes is due to the pancreas not producing enough insulin, which is needed to regulate blood glucose levels. In the event of glucose levels becoming too high, organs, vessels and nerves can become damaged. Pupils with Type 1 diabetes will need to have their blood glucose levels regularly checked and most take daily insulin injections. It is imperative, as with any child, that pupils with Type 1 diabetes have a healthy diet and regular exercise. Type 2 diabetes is also a lifelong condition which causes a person's blood sugar level to become too high, and although most common in adults is now seen in increasing numbers of younger people, usually related to obesity but sometimes genetically determined (NHS, 2014).

'Hypos' (hypoglycaemia, or low blood glucose) are more likely to happen if pupils have:

- missed a meal or snack;
- their lunch is delayed;
- they have not had sufficient carbohydrate at their last meal;
- they have had strenuous exercise without additional carbohy-drates or lowering their insulin;
- they have an intercurrent illness, e.g. a cold.

(Diabetes UK, 2014)

Commons signs of a hypo are:

- feeling shaky;
- sweating and increased heart rate;
- hunger;
- tiredness;
- blurred vision;
- pins and needles around the mouth;
- finding it hard to concentrate or feeling tearful;
- being stubborn and stroppy.

These are just some of the symptoms of a hypo; everyone is different and not all signs may be displayed. It is important to check with parents and – with their consent – with the diabetes nurse specialist for the individual pupil, who should have a written health care plan including information about what their own hypos might look like. If you have any concerns regarding a pupil's wellbeing, seek support from a qualified first-aider and if in doubt call for a paramedic ambulance.

The intention of this chapter was to provide you with some key information on some areas of exceptionality that you are likely to come across in your teaching careers. It is essential that you find out the information about the needs of the individual pupils in your class, their care plans and support requirements.

Key questions to consider

- Who can give me the information I need on the pupils I will teach?
- What systems exist in the context I am in to liaise with the pupil's parents/carers and wider family?
- Am I enabling the pupils to participate fully in the learning I am providing through knowing and understanding their particular needs?
- Are there any specific access requirements I need to consider, such as classroom layout, seating and acoustics?
- Have I planned specifically to remove barriers to learning for individual pupils?
- If I am using the Internet to find out about a particular area of need, how can I be sure it is a credible source?

Additional resources

As well as the resources you'll find at **www.sagepub.co.uk/martindenham** you should also take a look at the following:

Contact a Family, www.cafamily.org.uk: This website is an extensive source of information. It is useful if you need to find out about the particular aspects of a diagnosed condition such as prevalence, inheritance patterns, treatment, symptoms and for signposting to charities and further information.

Council for Disabled Children, www.councilfordisabledchildren.org.uk: This website contains lots of useful information and guidance for professionals and parents of disabled children and young people.

Diabetes UK www.diabetes.org.uk: The charity cares for, connects with and campaigns on behalf of those affected by and at risk of diabetes. The website provides extensive information and guidance with news and updates.

Disability Matters, www.disabilitymatters.org.uk: This is a suite of free e-learning resources produced by a consortium of partners across agencies, together with children with disabilities, young people, parents, carers and the voluntary sector, led by the Royal College of Paediatrics and Child Health, UK. The resources cover a range of issues to do with disability, with lots of ideas on how to make reasonable adjustments.

Genetic Disorders UK, www.geneticdisordersuk.org: A charity organisation who also run the Genes Day fundraising event. The website content is contributed to by those with personal experiences of living with genetic disorders.

SWAN UK, http://undiagnosed.org.uk Please refer parents and carers to this website if they have a child with an undiagnosed genetic condition.

The National Health Service (NHS) (2014), www.nhs.uk: The Health A–Z on the website is particularly useful as it provides information and guidance on a range of health difficulties including diseases and syndromes. There are also video clips from those who are living with particular areas of exceptionality.

Unique – The Rare Chromosome Disorder Support Group, www. rarechromo.co.uk: This website is used by clinical geneticists and provides a very useful source of validated information for professionals and parents about a range of chromosomal disorders.

Possible solutions

For the Reflective activity on p. 145

There will be specific sessions in the Disability Matters e-learning resource that are focussed on celebrating diversity. There are also many more easily accessible websites which provide suggestions of how to celebrate difference across the age phases.

CHAPTER 13

PROMOTING POSITIVE BEHAVIOUR

Bill Ashton

Key ideas explored in this chapter

- Common reasons why children and young people display challenging and unco-operative behaviours
- The impact of early years' trauma and loss
- Preparing to teach pupils with challenging behaviour
- Managing extreme behaviours in mainstream schools and specialist provision
- Useful strategies to manage behaviour in specialist provision
- Strategies, techniques and consistent approaches
- Changing challenging behaviour
- What is Team-Teach?

Common reasons why children display challenging and unco-operative behaviours

There are numerous reasons why children of all ages present with challenging behaviours; these may include tiredness, hunger, boredom or to seek attention. Some behaviours are simply children trying to understand the rules of new contexts, and testing boundaries is a natural part of their development. However, some children are unco-operative as they have experienced relational trauma and or/ loss. Others will be represented by those who have experienced inconsistent parenting especially during the early years of develop-ment. The earlier the trauma and or/loss, the more inconsistent the parenting the greater the effect on the child's perception of the world and their ability to form future relationships with peers and adults. The behaviours of children who are challenging, unco-operative or withdrawn and unsociable should not be interpreted lightly. These behaviours are actually complex and form a communication from which we must try to make sense if we are to manage them sensitively and effectively.

The impact of early years' trauma and loss

Trauma or loss in the early years can include mental health problems of parents, witnessing or hearing domestic violence, neglect, physi-cal abuse, sexual abuse, broken attachments with parents and key family members and bereavement. Children who are fostered or who are in residential care may have experienced many of the above on a regular basis. With so many unresolved issues it is inevitable that they will be expressed in behaviours that are difficult to interpret and manage. In the end the term 'challenging behaviour' refers to a range of behaviours that present as a problem to others, not some-thing intrinsic to the child. They represent the greatest of unmet needs. For ourselves working in mainstream schools or specialist provision it is important that we learn to take a professional approach to the understanding and response to the wide range of challenging behaviours. In the end by doing it right we can be powerful agents of change for the better.

 Key points to remember

- The earlier the traumas and/or loss, the greater the potential for harm to the child's development.
- Children may present on many different levels as much as younger than their peers. That is because some parts of the brain have a maturity lag.

(Continued)

(Continued)

- Memories are stored in a very complex system around cognitive and sensory formats. Whatever the age of trauma, the brain is able to remember it.
- The part of the brain that has responsibility for empathy, cause and effect and logic is the frontal cortex. It is this part that is likely to suffer a defect as a result of early years' trauma or inconsistent parenting.
- Many children become hard-wired for self-protection. In the early years the brain may have become hyper-vigilant against threat. This may remain in later years and can interfere significantly with behaviours and learning.
- Teachers and support staff who develop strong relationships with these children can either confirm or challenge what has gone before. We need to disappoint their brains by challenging what has happened to them.
- The brain is changing throughout life and can change positively with understanding teachers who can also listen and nurture. The earlier we intervene, the more chance of good, satisfying learning outcomes.

Preparing to teach pupils with challenging behaviour

Initial teacher training will have exposed you to theories around teaching and learning which should give you an insight into effective strategies to use in the classroom. Inevitably they fall short as they are rarely based on the experience of skilled practitioners. What works with one group of pupils may fail with another very different group. When you are given a group of pupils to teach for the first time in your new job they are all yours, so it is of vital importance that you employ tried and tested strategies.

The following strategies are worth considering:

- Smile and appear confident (even if to start with you are not feeling smiley or confident).
- In the classroom position yourself so that you have sight of every pupil.
- Find out as much as you can about the pupils you are teaching from their previous teachers and school records. Try to ignore 'unprofessional remarks' about their learning or behaviours.

- As far as possible have a layout in your classroom that is best suited to your teaching style and the subject being taught. Your classroom should be kept tidy with attention paid to purposeful, interactive and up-to-date displays.
- Ensure that you are familiar with and adhere to the school's behaviour management policy and that you know the roles of key staff who support the policy.

CASE STUDY

Managing low-level disruptive behaviours

For a number of years I struggled with teaching groups of children who presented with moderate and at times extremely challenging behaviours. It eventually became apparent that it was my behaviour that needed to change. Shortly after my revelation I discovered the work of Bill Rogers. I attended a training seminar and I watched his videos, which were amusing and uplifting in the way he described simple and practical ideas to use with a wide range of situations. From those early days to now, I continue to use many of the techniques espoused by him.

Broadly speaking you need to:

- appear confident with your classroom management strategies, conveying clearly and concisely your expectations. Some pupils will inevitably take advantage of slip-ups or indecision.
- be assertive and transparently fair, making it clear that transgressions of reasonable expectations will be calmly responded to. If criticism is to be used it must apply to the action/behaviour and not to be personalised in any way.
- give regular, constructive feedback and praise whenever appropriate. If we are praised (which is not often) we feel very good, and so do children. Take care not to patronise.

If you are to promote positive behaviours with pupils who are inclined to be disruptive and at times extremely challenging, you need to use a finer set of tools. In order to improve their behaviour there needs to be an ethos of 'positive correction' by adopting a non-confrontational approach to managing negative behaviours. This is based on a respect for the rights and dignity of children as individuals, allowing them to make choices about the consequences of their activities which encourage them to begin to self-regulate and correct their behaviour. Self-regulation is the ultimate goal for a child.

Remember at the start of a lesson to:

- greet the pupils at the door and welcome them by name into the classroom. It is important that you direct them to where they are sitting with clear instructions. Managing these transitions well will ensure they are quickly settled and ready for learning.
- ensure that all pupils are ready for learning before you begin your lesson. This can be achieved by giving concise instructions/praise such as 'Good sitting, James', 'Suta, listen', 'Eyes and ears this way everyone'.

 Key points to remember

- You must not begin teaching until the class is giving you their full attention.
- If you ignore a disruption (e.g. rising noise levels and talking), then it will be deemed to be acceptable to individuals or the group. Talk about the expectations in the context you are in, in accordance with the school's behaviour management policy.

When the class/group are working you need to re-affirm your expectations and respond to low-level behaviours to reduce the likelihood of more extreme behaviours happening. To do this you need to be aware of triggers that certain pupils may have which cause them anxiety or distress. If you are aware of the triggers you will be able to put steps into place to address their barriers to learning. If you have a child who is demonstrating disruptive behaviours you could try to use a holding strategy, described below.

CASE STUDY

A holding strategy

A pupil in the class has come into the lesson unsettled and is calling another pupil names. The pupil is looking around the classroom to see if his friends are impressed with what he is saying. You need to approach the pupil, take them to one side of the classroom (preferably out of view of their peers), get down to their level so that your faces are at the same level. Quietly tell the pupil that their behaviour is unacceptable and you will talk to them at the end of the lesson. Tell them that if the behaviour continues you will take further action (in line with the school's behaviour management policy of the context). This strategy can be effective as it removes the audience from the pupil and allows you to deal with the situation one-to-one. It also allows you to focus on the individual aside from the rest of the class.

Your use of language is really important in maintaining an environment that is conducive to teaching and learning. If you use negative language such as 'You are all too noisy', 'You are all off task', 'You are just unable to behave' you will not change the behaviours. Instead use positive language such as 'I'd like you all to stop, look at me and listen, thank you.' This can be reinforced with counting back 5, 4, 3, 2, 1, shaking a musical instrument (particularly effective with younger children). When giving out instructions or a direction whilst pupils are working, wait for several seconds for it to register. With young primary age children it may appear that they are ignoring you. They are simply absorbing the request before registering it and usually ... responding!

Managing extreme behaviours in mainstream schools and specialist provision

Extreme behaviours can take a number of forms depending on the group and the setting, including biting, nipping, spitting, kicking and fighting. In mainstream schools these tend to emerge with a very troubled child or when a small group of children with complex lives are put together as a class. Most of the extremely challenging behaviour is acted out in special units such as a pupil referral unit (PRU) or in a specialist context for children with emotional, social and behavioural difficulties (ESBD). In well-led units and specialist provision extremely challenging behaviour, whilst being the norm, is well managed, taking into account the triggers, individual needs and expected responses of the pupil. The staff usually receive appropriate training and their emotional wellbeing is catered for by way of peer support and good management guidance.

In some settings, particularly PRUs, the management of behaviours is often left to the personal skills or positive attitude of individual members of staff. Despite some good leadership, PRUs are often under-resourced and specialist training and a collegiate approach are fragmented.

 Key points to remember

- Discover any trigger points and have a quick response to signs of anxiety or tension such as rocking, tapping, refusing to co-operate and/or withdrawing from the group.
- Apply the practice around being a good role model.
- Look out for early signs of negative behaviours so that you can attempt to de-escalate.
- Ensure that you know and understand the behaviour management policy of the school and the key people who are responsible for supporting the policy.

Useful strategies to manage behaviour in specialist provision

First and foremost, it is better to try to predict a behaviour or behaviours and to intervene early to divert or defuse it. You will learn through experience and honest reflective practice to identify the subtle indicators that enable you to smoothly change the course of potentially damaging behaviours. With behaviours that challenge us, we need to remind ourselves that as human beings we can react naturally to behaviours from others. As professionals, it is important for us to take a step back both emotionally and physically when challenging behaviours arise. We must control the reaction to our feelings so that we do not feed the conflict from a child or a group of children. You can manage the behaviour of others by quickly assessing situations and then influencing behaviours by controlling and managing your responses.

It is worth reminding ourselves that most behaviours are driven by our subconscious; that is, they are learned. If that is the case, most of the extremely challenging behaviours exhibited by children are embedded within them. In spite of knowing this some teachers and support staff will say 'He knows what he is doing' – really?

There are a range of strategies you can employ in response to early stage challenging behaviours from pupils:

- Display very calm body language.
- Let them know you are aware and that the behaviour is unacceptable and/or concerning.

- Reassure them and ask if they want to talk.
- Divert and distract them in an attempt to resolve the behaviours.

There will be times when the pupils you are teaching display high-level behaviours. The indicators of these could be one or some of the following: displaying tension, making personal remarks, talking loudly, calling out, aggressive posture, being destructive, picking up objects, pacing and hurting others or themselves.

In response to these behaviours you could begin by trying some of the lower-level behaviour techniques discussed earlier in the chapter. As a trainee teacher it is vital that you keep yourself safe and allow the adults employed by the setting to take charge of high-level behaviours.

 Reflective activity

As a newly qualified teacher you have been given a group of 14 Year 4 (age 7–8 years) pupils. You have the necessary information regarding their levels of attainment. As you progress into the early part of the lesson, one of the boys begins to flick his near neighbour's equipment on to the floor and take objects from a pencil case and throw them on to the floor. When you draw his attention to you and ask him to stop, he pauses for a couple of minutes and then continues similar behaviours.

Consider your reaction to this situation. How should you respond? How might you plan to prevent these behaviours happening again? (Some suggestions are given at the end of the chapter.)

When the behaviours have subsided, allow the pupil to return to the class.

Some common strategies used to de-escalate extreme behaviours are:

- Remain calm and if necessary send a trusted pupil to get further support.
- Clearly state the expected standards of behaviour.
- Offer alternatives and options ('You can stop or go to the chill-out room').
- Provide a get-out without criticism, using concise language.

Following extreme challenging behaviour what you have planned to teach may have been lost. What matters now is that the pupil can recover with dignity, without blame and offering support when they are ready to talk (which may take some time).

Key points to remember

- LISTEN – this will give you an indication of the pupils' moods and feelings.
- Contain your anxiety and keep calm.
- Respond to the child, not the challenging behaviour.
- Acknowledge compliance, ignore the challenge.
- DON'T enter into battles you cannot win.
- Make praise specific: say *what* they've done well rather than just a general 'You're doing great'.
- The worse the level of behaviour, the smaller the sanctions (think carefully about this).
- Don't shout.
- Don't make threats like 'You do this, I will (or won't) do that'.

Strategies, techniques and constant approaches

If you have predictable and constant responses to unwanted behaviour you will promote a positive representation of you as a safe haven. This is vital if you want to bring about change for the future.

Planned ignoring

This can often be misunderstood and badly misapplied. If a child feels they are being ignored, they have lots of strategies to get your attention. Most of these behaviours inevitably make the situation worse. Therefore we can ignore the behaviour but not the child, remaining sensitive to unmet needs. However, planned ignoring can be very effective. It is the unwanted behaviour that is ignored, not the child. There are some important aspects to consider when using planned ignoring:

- Take no notice of behaviours such as rude remarks and protests.
- Give the child a reassuring message without commenting on their behaviour, for example 'I will come over to you but I need you to stop kicking the table and chairs first.'
- Time limit your behaviour above by returning to give them attention. This will appear forgiving, which is not what the child expects.
- Try to get on with supporting other children or some other activity while the above is going on. At the same time turn and show the child a gesture or smile that shows you recognise that they are still there.

Time-limited removal

This can work well for relatively low-level difficulties that do not need a lengthy intervention. It provides removal from the reinforcers without generating feelings of rejection. The pupil should be removed to a space nearby with a time limit on the removal (say three minutes); you should remain in sight and reasonable proximity to the child. You should remain sensitive to their mood, ignoring the behaviour. Once the time is up, acknowledge that the pupil has been co-operative and return them to the group in a positive way. This can be repeated but it needs to be done sensitively, carefully reading the signs from their body language. If the child tries to engage during the time-limited removal you should employ attentive silence, give a head nod or hand gesture. If the child continues, simply look at them and say 'three minutes', keep doing this calmly and quietly until you gain compliance. Do not add on time.

Time-in

Time with you if you can give it is a valuable tool, even if used for a few minutes. You can explain why things are not working and the pupil can have an opportunity to describe their feelings. You should do this in a non-judgemental way.

Reporting incidents

When a pupil's behaviour causes serious disruption to a lesson in either a mainstream or a specialist context, it is important to try to understand the reasons for the behaviours. You will be required to communicate an outline of the build-up and events to a member of the team. In most settings and depending on other factors, such as if this is a new behaviour for the pupil, there may be a debrief with the senior management team and the parents/carers will be informed. There will be a review of the event and the actions taken. In most cases there will be an agreed plan to limit or reduce the likelihood of a similar event re-occurring.

Behaviour modification charts

It is important to recognise that behaviour that is modified by way of rewards and sanctions may reappear in other forms, as underlying behaviours have not changed and are still embedded. Having said that, behaviour modification charts can, if used constructively, help with changing or moderating negative behaviours.

Star charts

A star chart is a simple, visual chart that allows a pupil to see progress towards agreed goals. Stars or symbols of interest are added to the chart as small steps are completed towards what must be tangible rewards. Young children especially enjoy this approach and it also serves to break the cycle of nagging by converting to positivity. When using charts you need to ensure that they are age appropriate, considering their chronological and developmental ages. You need to ensure that the pupil can achieve your expectations and they are supported and reminded of these. You need to be consistent in when you hand out the stickers, and never take those away that have been awarded. Reward systems are a useful way to raise self-esteem and to accept and learn from consequences. You need to be aware that not all pupils will be motivated by star charts; their negative behaviours could possibly be aggravated by frustration and lack of success.

The traffic light system

The name 'traffic light' comes from combining a simple diagram and the symbolic use of red, amber and green. In many cases children may want to use other symbols. The traffic light system does offer rewards, but it is primarily a method that works on longer-term interventions. They are for communicating a pupil's behaviour and to promote reflection. This system does not rely on the pupil having controls, nor does it require the motivation of the child in the same way. Traffic lights provide the opportunity to give rewards for good behaviour and to sanction unwanted behaviour. The sanctions are actually the colour itself. It is important that the child understands and agrees to the system. The traffic light system can be used with individual pupils, groups or the whole class and is an effective approach for all ages.

The traffic light system allows three scores:

- Met expectations (green)
- Met expectations with support (amber)
- Did not meet expectations (red)

This means the pupil should not feel that they have failed over small issues. The key idea is that they will accept support and work to meet expectations.

It is vital that teachers and support staff are consistent in the way that the scores are applied. The traffic light system offers an opportunity to gain rewards and it allows for a shared monitoring of the child's behaviour. A value is given to each light colour: green (3), amber (2) and red (0). You can have a number of forms of traffic lights operating. For example, in a primary school or a fixed group, they can be used to monitor behaviour throughout the day. In secondary schools or schools where there is a regular change of lessons throughout the day, the system can be used in subject areas where challenging behaviours have been identified. Pastoral leaders can also use the system as a tool for changing behaviours. As long as there is consistency, the system is flexible.

Changing challenging behaviour

Pupil-centred and effective interventions can be developed and introduced to encourage change towards improved behaviour. The emphasis must be on communication with children and their active involvement in the change process. In some mainstream schools, ESBD approaches to challenging behaviours are rooted in social learning theory. These approaches reward wanted positive behaviours through privileges and rewards, and remove privileges or apply sanctions for unwanted negative behaviours. This approach may be effective if children are able to self-regulate and can adapt to this way of working. However, pupils who lack sound inner controls tend to be disorganised and are likely to mistrust what appears to be a straightforward system for improving behaviour.

Many challenging behaviours can be seen as rooted in unmet needs, often resulting in poor inhibitions and lack of impulse control. The outcome of this is that a pupil will not change their behaviour just because we want them to and we have rewarded them when they conform. These pupils who may be endlessly corrected are likely to believe that they are always wrong and can do very little that is right. This means that their very identity will appear to them to be under attack and they will either withdraw into themselves or retaliate aggressively. Some pupils who have developed very weak attachments because of early life trauma will seek out attention no matter how negative it is. Confrontation is a guaranteed way of gaining attention.

Perhaps it is better to accept modifying unwanted behaviours than to attempt to remove them completely. By focussing on those behaviours that matter we may be able to make progress more effectively than trying to change them all. We are fallible and we can be drawn into conflict and a battle of wills with some pupils. Avoid any sense of the pupil being wrong, it is their behaviour that is the issue. We need to build their confidence so that they will collaborate with us.

What is Team-Teach?

Team-Teach is a programme dedicated to the behaviour support, intervention and de-escalation of challenging behaviours. It was first devised in the UK by George Matthews who, as a teacher, was keen to support staff in developing de-escalation skills which allow 95 per cent of situations in schools and specialist provision to be defused without physical intervention. Over two decades this programme has been developed into one of the largest training providers in behaviour support and management, including physical intervention. Team-Teach is now advised and supported by experts in the field of education and managers of a range of services for children and adults with often severe and challenging difficulties. The focus of Team-Teach is primarily around keeping people safe whilst supporting their learning of better ways to manage their behaviour. When used properly, the methods of de-escalation and in rare cases physical restraint are worthwhile and an important tool in the management of significant challenging behaviours.

Additional resources

As well as the resources you'll find at **www.sagepub.co.uk/martindenham** you should also take a look at the following:

Geddes, H. (2006) *Attachment in the Classroom: The Link Between Children's Early Experience, Emotional Wellbeing and Performance in School*. London: Worth. This book is essential reading for teachers, support staff and parents/carers as it examines the causes of the difficulties with practical advice to support the child.

Rogers, B. (2011) *You Know The Fair Rule: Strategies for Positive and Effective Behaviour Management and Discipline in Schools*. London: Pearson. This book is recommended as it is a comprehensive, practical, and realistic guide to effective practice in managing behaviour. It acknowledges and addresses the challenges faced by teachers in dealing with behaviour patterns and issues, and provides practical advice.

Rogers, B. and McPherson, E. (2014) *Behaviour Management with Young Children: Crucial First Steps with Children 3–7 Years*, 2nd edn. London: SAGE. This book shares a range of strategies and techniques to manage transitions, develop trust, support children with ESBD and communicate effectively with parents and carers.

Yellow Kite: Attachment Support Service for Schools, www.theyellowkite.co.uk: This website identifies and promotes ways of improving inclusion for pupils with attachment difficulties.

Possible solutions

For the Reflective activity on p. 157

If there is a TA in the room, ask them to sit next to the pupil to see if that modifies his behaviour. If you are alone and the pupils are working, you can try two options. The first is to sit next to the pupil and support him with his work as a distraction to his disruption. The second is to call him by name and ask him to come and talk to you, or if it is more appropriate you go to him. Describe the behaviour you want him to stop and remind him of what you would like him to do. If the behaviour continues you should ask him to sit in another part of the room, preferably with you. Use this time as an opportunity for him to calm down, giving him the opportunity to talk to you about the reasons for the behaviour.

CHAPTER 14

HOW TO WORK EFFECTIVELY WITH SUPPORT STAFF AND OTHER PROFESSIONALS

Judith Donovan and Pauline James

Key ideas explored in this chapter

- The role and responsibilities of support staff
- The experience and qualities of the support staff and what they bring to a setting
- How to effectively deploy support staff
- How to work effectively with other professionals

The role and responsibilities of support staff

In a specialist context it is crucial that you are knowledgeable about the role and responsibilities of the individual support staff whom you are working with. There are, in general terms, three levels of support staff: unqualified support staff, whose primary role is changing and feeding pupils; a nursery nurse or classroom assistant, who will have a level 2 or 3 qualification (equivalent to GCSE or A-level); and the higher level teaching assistant (HLTA), who will be qualified at level 4 (the first year of an under-graduate degree). Some HLTAs are responsible for the day-to-day running of classes under the guidance of the teacher, while others are responsible for a particular subject area or aspect such as moving and handling or behaviour. Quite often level 2 assistants will be directed in their role by a level 3 or 4 assistant, who in turn is directed by the teacher. Support staff may be given alternative titles such as Special Needs Assistant (SNA) or Child Care Worker.

Support staff are the thread that pulls together all of the different aspects of learning and care that take place so that the pupils are able to progress. The role of support staff is wide and varied, depending on the setting, but generally they will help pupils to access the learning offered by supporting them in whichever way is necessary. In the simplest of terms, this will be with academic work (under the supervision of the teacher), but may involve helping a pupil to use their PECS® book, understand a visual timetable, program a touch talker, or facilitate the Task Series in Conductive Education. As the class teacher you are responsible for working with the pupil on a daily basis. To do this effectively you need to work collaboratively with support staff to plan and assess the impact of support and interventions.

In summary, the main responsibilities of support staff are to:

- support the teacher in providing effective learning opportunities for their pupils;
- prepare resources, displays and organise the classroom;
- attend to any care needs pupils may have;
- have a knowledge and understanding of child development, teaching strategies, curriculum, behaviour management and assessment;
- be an essential part of the school/class team;
- be responsible for health care needs and all areas of personal, social and health education (PSHE), which generally threads through all areas of the special school curriculum;
- form strong bonds with both pupils and parents/carers;
- work with small groups and individuals to further their learning and development and report learning and progress to the class teacher.

The focus of the work of support staff is to build self-esteem, to encourage pupils to be confident and independent, to understand what is expected of them and to ensure that their care needs are met. Support staff may be involved in facilitating pre-set therapy programmes (physiotherapy, occupational therapy, rebound therapy, hydrotherapy), give medication and have knowledge of medical management plans, and are often a consummate source of knowledge in the classroom. They will be involved in behaviour modification techniques and often have particular responsibilities for which they have been trained. They will prepare learning materials, keep records and in some cases write in the home-school diary. Some support staff may be bi-lingual and an essential resource for teaching and supporting pupils with EAL.

The experience and qualities of the support staff and what they bring to a setting

Support staff are, generally, hard-working, dedicated and caring people. They are usually well trained and want to be effective. They are patient and very perceptive. In support staff you have a wealth of knowledge and experience that can make your role much easier. Support staff can bring an added dimension to the classroom; they have a different world view to the teacher and see learning from a totally alternative but complementary perspective. They are the essential link between care and education and enable learning related to the whole child.

When a group of support staff were asked how they like to be treated in school they said:

- Treat us with respect.
- Treat us as an equal as we do have knowledge.
- We like to be asked rather than told.
- Tell us what we need to do in class, initially, and what information it will be helpful for us to provide.
- Ask us for help and to share what we know.
- Allow clear communication from both sides at the beginning of the lesson.
- Discuss lesson plans and we will work with ideas.
- Ask us if things need doing so we know what we can do to support.
- Acknowledge when we have done something well and celebrate our successes.

How to effectively deploy support staff

A thorough knowledge of the classroom setting and the needs of all pupils is essential in order to effectively deploy support staff. Very often they will be highly experienced in their current role and be able to offer sound, valuable advice on effective classroom management and what individual pupils need. Respect is the key, both respect for the person and respect for their considerable knowledge, but it is also important that support staff know that it is you who will ultimately make any decisions that have to be made. Start in the way you mean to go on, be firm but considerate, include support staff in all of your discussions about learning, ask for their opinion, listen and learn. Support staff need to have ownership of the learning that takes place and to feel valued. In a classroom for pupils with severe and complex needs there can sometimes be up to eight support staff. Obviously they are highly specialised and it can be difficult to know how to direct them. You can assign them to specific pupils, but they need to be rotated if the pupil is very demanding. You are responsible for their wellbeing as well as your own. Use their strengths; they are trained in specific areas, so use them accordingly.

 Reflective activity

You are working with a Key Stage 5 class of pupils with SLD. You have one senior support assistant (SSA) and one support assistant (SA) working with you in the class. The SSA is much older than you, and has been at the school for a long time. On a number of occasions while you are teaching, she has contradicted you in front of the pupils. When it comes to her time to leave she just puts down what she is doing and leaves, not clearing up any mess she has left. What would you do? (Some suggestions are given at the end of the chapter.)

Teachers and training teachers are responsible for deploying their support staff effectively. This can be a challenge, particularly if they have more experience than you. You will need to plan for the pupils' learning collaboratively, sharing ideas and considering what the pupils' needs and targets are. It is essential that you present your lesson plans in advance of the session so they have an opportunity to ask you any questions and clarify any aspects which they feel are unclear. They need to comprehend what you are setting out to achieve in any intervention or activity that has a focus on moving the pupil on. Always be fair when delegating pupils/activities to the support staff. Don't give them the most challenging group every time, share pupils across the staff. This is also essential for promoting independence as it is not good practice for pupils to become reliant upon a particular member of the team.

⌐⌐ Key points to remember

- You must respect your support staff and you must gain their respect. You will need to ask their advice, listen to what they say whilst remaining the lead figure.
- You will need to establish consistent approaches. To do this you will need to be certain that the support staff fully understand what it is you expect from the lesson, the learning outcome, success criteria and the activity.
- Support staff must be clear about who they are expected to work with or what you want their role to be.
- Consider the best ways to share your lesson plans with support staff. Ask the class teacher what he/she does, give support staff time to read the lesson plan, discuss the lesson before the pupils come into class or write a plan for the day/lesson highlighting which member of support staff you would like to work with which pupils.
- You must always have secure knowledge of the subject/skill you are going to teach. You need to be sure that the support staff have also been supported to understand the processes you are teaching.
- You need to decide how learning, achievements or misconceptions will be reported to you at the end of a lesson to ensure that you can take the learning forward and revisit ideas.
- Talk about 'we' as you are all one team, and don't ever say 'just' a member of the support team!

As a leader within your class you are to some extent responsible for the development of your staff team. It is hoped that most support staff in specialist schools will be highly skilled. However, when you begin teaching the class you will have skills and ideas they may not be familiar with. You must make sure they fully understand the skill you are trying to teach the pupils. This is where you need to make sure that the support staff fully understand the learning outcome of the lesson, because at the end of it you need to know whether the pupil mastered the skill and if not what they will need to do to promote achievement. As you will seldom be teaching all the pupils together all of the time you will rely on the support staff to give you this information.

As a trainee teacher you will equally rely on the support staff to give you information about prior learning as well as about the individual pupils, many of whom may have complex difficulties. It would be beneficial to both you and your support staff if you could tactfully encourage them to consider certain aspects of the lesson, as given below.

Key questions for support staff to consider at the end of a lesson

- How well did the pupils understand/achieve what they were expected to do?
- Were the pupils able to concentrate throughout the lesson?
- Did I give opportunities for speaking, listening and talk?
- Did I promote independence when possible?
- Were successes celebrated?
- Have I fed back the learning and progress to the teacher?

 Reflective activity

Consider the following comments which have been given by support staff following an activity. Comment on the quality of the feedback given. Does it give you sufficiently detailed information to inform your next steps for the pupil? What would make it better? How can you ensure that your support staff will be able to give appropriate and effective feedback?

1. Tariq worked well and tried hard. He could do elements of the task with support.
2. Hugh maintained concentration throughout the activity and was able to count 1 to 10 consistently with all three attempts. He touched each bear as he counted them. To challenge him I then set out 12 bears, which he was able to count reliably on 2/3 occasions.
3. Task completed.
4. Jenny was able to turn the pages of the book *The Hungry Caterpillar* and held it the correct way up (P4 achieved). I have noted this in her assessment evidence. The activity will need to be repeated for JC and PT as they were uninterested for the majority of the activity. Maybe we could look at different books/devices to see if we can find content they are motivated by?

Reflective activity

You have been asked to work in a class where the support assistant insists on working with only one pupil – a pupil who he feels comfortable with. This pupil is difficult to motivate and responds well to the support assistant. You have directed him to work with a variety of pupils but he is always found to be working with this particular child. He has even re-deployed support assistants (level 2) within the class so that he can continue to work with this pupil. What would you do in this situation? (Some suggestions are given at the end of the chapter.)

How to work effectively with other professionals

During your placement in special educational provision you will come across and work alongside many of the following professions: social services, child and adolescent mental health services (CAMHS), occupational therapists, speech therapists, physiotherapists, visually impaired specialists, improving progressions team, educational psychologists, community nursing team, behaviour groups, orthotics, consultant paediatricians, epilepsies nurse, welfare rights, looked after team, nursing disability team, pets as therapy dog and owner. An outline of the majority of these roles can be found in Chapter 2. These services exist to support the pupils, their families and the school in facilitating their individual needs. The key points below are useful in working with other professionals.

 Key points to remember

- Offer them professional courtesy – remember they are the experts in their field.
- Don't be afraid to ask so that you gain a better understanding of their role if you are unclear.
- Try to remember their names and which service they are by making a note as soon as possible after they have left.
- Use them as a resource, learn from them and value what they say.
- Be specific about what you want to know when working with them.

- Remember that we should all be working together for the benefit of the child.
- Get information about how to contact them before they leave the school.

It is important to remember that schools could not run efficiently without a team-based approach. It is hoped that the guidance in this chapter will facilitate effective working relationships with you and the team you are working with.

Additional resources

As well as the resources you'll find at **www.sagepub.co.uk/martindenham** you should also take a look at the following:

Times Education Supplement (TES connect), http://www.tes.co.uk/ teaching-assistants-whole-school-teaching-resources/: This website has a wealth of resources on behaviour, EAL and lesson ideas, which can be accessed by class teachers and support staff. By entering 'teaching assistants' into the search on the website you can find extensive information on all aspects of how to work effectively as a team to raise standards.

Possible solutions

For the Reflective activity on p. 167

Discuss the situation with the teacher and ask for their advice as they will know this person better than you. If they think you should tackle the situation and you feel confident, choose a time of day when you are alone. Ask her if she could not interrupt you during the lesson as you feel it disturbs the pupils' learning and it is confusing for them to understand who is in charge of the class. Suggest that she notes down any corrections she feels you need to make so that you can address them following the lesson. In terms of not tidying up, you could begin by supporting the tidying up and doing it together. This time could be used to show you value her contributions and efforts during the school day.

(Continued)

(Continued)

For the Reflective activity on p. 170

You could change the pattern of which member of the support staff team will be working with which group. Explain to them that you will be working with the demotivated pupil because you want to improve their participation. Ask the support assistant if he could use his skills to support different pupils across a series of lessons. Continue to modify who works with which pupil to ensure that the skills of the team are utilised with the different pupils; this will also reduce over-dependency.

CHAPTER 15

SUPPORTING LEARNING IN A PUPIL REFERRAL UNIT (PRU)

Steve Siddell

Key ideas explored in this chapter

- Why do we have PRUs and do they make sense?
- Why do pupils go to PRUs?
- What is it like to be a pupil in a PRU?
- What is it like to be a teacher in a PRU?

Why do we have PRUs and do they make sense?

Pupil referral units (PRUs) are typically for pupils who have been permanently excluded from a mainstream school. They vary considerably, some doing referral work for those close to exclusion, others brokering alternative provision arrangements.

The Department for Education (DfE, 2014a) describes two types of exclusion: fixed period (suspended) and permanent (expelled). A fixed period exclusion is where a pupil is temporarily removed from school for up to 45 days in a school year. A permanent exclusion means the pupil is expelled permanently. You may also hear of 'home and hospital' provisions, and although some of these are PRUs they are very different in their nature and support students who are 'unable to attend school on health grounds'. In this context health grounds may describe a broken leg, a life-threatening disease or emotional/mental health needs. They are very different from the PRUs for the excluded and as such are not considered here.

So, why do we have PRUs? Ask this question in any mainstream school staffroom and you are likely to hear no shortage of theories from talk of 'poverty and bad parenting' to the 'hang 'em and flog 'em' brigade. You can learn a great deal about the real ethos of a school by listening to the specific language in use. Think about this in your own context: do you hear terms such as 'internal exclusion', 'expelled' (an old term still in use), 'isolation', 'remove', 'on report'?

Does this language suggest a culture which believes in inclusion or the capacity of individuals to change? Does it support or hinder change? Does it suggest that behaviour is a problem for the young person or just the school?

You will meet colleagues during your career who are confused about the purpose of schools, they imagine that they exist to provide work for teachers. If you are tempted to see yourself philosophically aligned with this group, please reflect carefully on the following and then go to work in another field, perhaps banking.

 Key points to remember

- Children are people.
- Some of them are cleverer than you.
- They may not care for your values or beliefs – why should they?

What you are much less likely to encounter in this hypothetical staffroom is any actual experience of *teaching* in a PRU environment. PRUs have been, for a very long time, *part* of a system for education in the UK, yet in reality very much *apart* from that system.

Consider the basic premise, place all of the most 'difficult' children in one small, typically under-resourced 'unit' and then wait for them to get better. Does this model make any sense to you? Can you think of an example, perhaps outside of education, where this approach works?

So we begin this chapter about teaching in PRUs with a fundamental question about the validity of the practice of isolating 'difficult' children. Do not be discouraged, PRU practice is changing
rapidly in the UK and generally for the better. PRUs need the best
of teachers – this has always been true, but they have not always
seen them. It would be nice to imagine that PRUs exist to best support pupils who are experiencing behaviour problems, and this is
certainly the most palatable way of looking at them. They may also
exist to serve another less agreeable purpose, which is a conse-
quence of our current system. Some pupils 'fail in our mainstream
schools', though who is failing whom is a theme we will return to.
At the very least, the perceived function of a PRU is confused and
this alone means that we should question their role in our education system.

Consider this: are PRUs in place to punish, segregate, offer therapy,
keep young people off the streets, give them 'a short sharp shock',
educate, return pupils to school? It could easily be a far longer list.
One thing is clear: as long as schools permanently exclude pupils,
there will be a need for some form of alternative education. Interest-
ingly the nature of alternative education seems poised to change dramatically with FE colleges, mindful of the Wolf Report 2013, and the
likely spread of studio schools and other 14–19 year developments
now jockeying for business.

 Key points to remember

- The old model of the PRU is highly questionable and needs to be
  scrutinised.
- Education in the UK is set for another round of change, perhaps
  fundamentally at 14–19 (at the time of writing there are 1 million
  unemployed under-25s and thousands of unfilled vacancies,
  particularly in engineering).
- Whatever happens, we need as a nation to improve the quality and
  diversity of alternative provision.

Why do pupils go to PRUs?

There is good published evidence on why pupils go to PRUs in *A Profile
of Pupil Exclusions in England* (DfE, 2012b), though the evidence is
getting a little dated as it ends with 2010 data. Here are some key
points, though readers are urged to view the document in more detail.

Key points to remember

- Most permanent exclusion is from the secondary sector (more than 50 per cent is for 13–14 year olds); in 2009/2010, 0.15 per cent of secondary pupils were excluded compared to just 0.02 per cent of primary pupils.
- The most common reason for permanent exclusion is 'persistent disruptive behaviour', at 29 per cent during this period.
- Boys are more likely to be excluded than girls (both fixed-term and permanently).
- Pupils with statements of SEN are far more likely to be excluded – think about this, pupils whose special needs have been recognised are still nine times as likely to be fixed-term excluded and seven times as likely to be permanently excluded.
- Pupils in receipt of free school meals (FSM), a measure of deprivation, are four times as likely to be permanently excluded.
- Key ethnic groups, travellers of Irish heritage, Black Caribbean and Gypsy/Roma see the highest levels of exclusion.
- In 2009/2010, only 15.8 per cent of permanently excluded pupils did not have one or more of the following characteristic: SEN, FSM or Black Caribbean.

The most common reason for permanent exclusion is 'persistent disruptive behaviour'. This describes the pupil who has poor social skills, is impulsive, is unable pick up social cues (adolescent boys are not strong on empathy!), probably has poor literacy skills and has learned that he (for it is probably a boy) hates schools and teachers except for Mr X whom he likes. He has not threatened anyone with a knife, has not smoked opium during an assembly, but he just will not 'see sense' and he *persistently* disrupts lessons. This pupil will have been warned, will have had intervention, and the school will have 'exhausted all possible strategies' so the head teacher will have had no choice but to exclude him 'with a heavy heart'. These are the lines you find in exclusion letters and school documentation. Depressingly, it is not unusual to meet primary head teachers who can tell you exactly which pupils will most likely be excluded once they meet the complex demands of secondary education. If we know who these children are when they are four or five, why do we end up excluding them ten years later?

Managing the permanently excluded is an expensive and statutory responsibility for local authorities. Early intervention in the primary sector is cheaper and more effective but non-statutory, so can be cut or neglected. Thresholds vary enormously; in one school, behaviour that down the road would mean permanent exclusion would instead result in meaningful and effective intervention. What PRUs receiving these children do not usually find is any serious attempt to find out *why* the child has 'bad behaviour'. A good PRU starts with this question and keeps asking it until the underlying issues are understood – how can you tackle a problem that you do not understand? How do you help a child understand and start to manage their own behaviour if you do not know their mother has just gone back into prison and that their behaviour changed dramatically when their grandmother died four years ago?

Reflect on the premise 'behaviour is a communication' and ask yourself 'Are we listening hard enough?'.

 Key points to remember

- The factors that result in one child, who is experiencing difficulty, being appropriately supported and another being excluded are predictable, but tragically the actual outcomes are subject to a high degree of random chance.
- Schools use exclusion to protect the rights of the other pupils, not the excluded child. If all children have a right to learn, what does this mean for those that are excluded?
- If you want to be excluded from school then have special needs, be a boy, be poor and preferably from one of the key ethnic groups.

It is the business of PRUs to understand why a child behaves the way they do, to 'see the reasons not the problems'.

What is it like to be a pupil in a PRU?

Ask this question and you will hear as many answers as there are pupils to speak to. Many much prefer it to being at school because the 'staff listen more'; some do not want to be anywhere and will be dismissive of all forms of education; some will be alarmed and confused at the behaviour of their peers; others will display anger, sorrow, anxiety or depression. For some the PRU will be the single constant in their life and a place of relative security. What is a shock is that few of them will want to return to mainstream school.

Put yourself in the shoes of a child arriving in a PRU. You will need to start by reviewing the profile of permanently excluded children and then use your imagination. You have probably had, at best, chaotic attachments since early childhood and you have probably lived in a home without books or a table at which your family shares its meals. Who are your significant role models? When you started primary school you were almost certainly 'behind the curve', other children in your reception class could already read! Nevertheless you probably enjoyed primary school and you liked your teachers. Towards the end you may have spent quite a lot of time out of class. At secondary school you are wrong-footed by the complexity, the large number of your teachers, each with different expectations (consistency in schools is so important but so hard to get right) and you have just lost your secure relationship with your primary teacher, the one that looked after the 'special small class'. Things will be going wrong and you will be gaining a bad reputation. By year 9 puberty has smacked you in the face and you have discovered a whole sub-culture to join as a new family. You have been warned, been excluded several times or been isolated, possibly given a 'fresh start' in another school and then you find yourself with no school but an instruction to attend a PRU.

The PRU news may be frightening, or for many a good result because several of your 'mates' are already there. You arrive labelled and excluded by your community and with a formidable reputation. You are in your own town or city but probably in a different neigh-bourhood (important to territorial children who spend a lot of time on their streets – a distinction invisible to staff who drive in from across town), and some of your new neighbours think 'children like that should be in a unit on an industrial estate, not next to decent people like us'.

Good luck! The quality of the relationships you are able to form with the staff in the PRU is going to shape your adult life. If you were in charge, what sort of staff would you hope to recruit?

 Key points to remember

- Children arrive in PRUs for many reasons and they all have different stories, each of which needs to be understood. Listen to the children even when it sounds like nonsense.
- Careful induction is really important and some head teachers would always advocate a home visit as a first step.

- Just as in mainstream schools there is a hidden curriculum often overlooked by staff, but the stakes are higher.
- The children may be 'difficult', but always remember that they are this way for understandable reasons.
- PRUs should have the highest standards for recruitment.

What is it like to be a teacher in a PRU?

The short answer is 'very demanding and very rewarding'. Before exploring this question, some advice: the experience depends as much on you as it does on the PRU. Some highly effective PRU teachers report not wanting to return to mainstream because it is too restrictive, even 'boring'; these are very different professionals to those who are happiest with a focussed and compliant classroom.

It has occasionally been the case that teachers apply because they are attracted by the additional SEN allowance, the very small classes and the belief that there might be less scrutiny of their teaching. Appointment of such staff would lead to a very negative experience for the pupils and the adult. PRU teaching is different, but it's definitely not easier. The small numbers of pupils mean that you will have less marking, there will be more support and very small groups, but you will also be doing a job that is very emotionally demanding and you cannot have 'bad days'. As a professional, whatever your personal demons may be they must be left in your car and replaced with a sincere smile for the pupils. After all, they are damaged and vulnerable and they have plenty of problems of their own without suffering from yours. If you can excuse the cliché, 'they don't care what you know until they know that you care'.

So if you are motivated to make a difference for these pupils run through this checklist.

Are you ...?

- ☐ Self-aware and reflective
- ☐ Calm in a crisis
- ☐ Caring and non-judgemental
- ☐ Resilient
- ☐ Stable and resolved as an adult
- ☐ Secure in your own life
- ☐ Resourceful and creative
- ☐ Clear about your motivation

There are some real advantages for the right teachers and you will certainly hone your craft – one argument for having PRU placements for interested trainee teachers! You will almost certainly have an opportunity to teach outside of your specialism (if this fills you with horror, skip to the end, it's not for you) and to teach children rather than stuff. There should be opportunity to be less prescriptive and more creative with the curriculum, which should be both broad and personalised. Whilst a good PRU will always have a strong focus on core subjects and transition routes, it may also be a place rich in creative curriculum solutions. You could engage in project-based learning, college-based courses, building a sweat lodge or sharing adventure activities with the children. Above all, be ready to laugh with them – humour is truly a great medicine and PRUs should be therapeutic, not penal.

Teaching is often collaborative and you will rarely be the only adult in the classroom so you need to relish the chance to team teach and be fleet of foot; if a plan is not working you need to be ready to shift direction quickly. You also need to spot issues arising before they happen and intervene subtly, which requires skill, practice and empathy. Above all, you need to build relationships with the children for whom attachment disorders are the most common factor. You need to be fair and firm, friendly but not 'their mate'. Each child needs at least one significant adult at school whom they trust or simply 'like'. A child with a network of trusted adults is a child who can take control and begin to change.

Reflect on the power that teachers have to change young minds. Few people cannot recall a teacher who made a significant difference to the way they thought or alternatively left a deep scar by making a thoughtless remark. This is a huge responsibility; we are members of a profession that directly shapes young minds, so if you are sceptical about this Google 'neuroplasticity'.

Whilst many would argue that PRU children have failed in mainstream education, a more instructive view might be to consider that our systems have failed the child. What we know when a child comes into a PRU is that replicating a rigorous school model will not work, but we must also resist absolutely the informal model of 'drop in for a cup of tea and a game of ping pong'. Here lies the challenge – somewhere between these canonical extremes there is an optimal if dynamic balance. As teachers in a PRU we must pull off a clever trick of learning by stealth and keep a constant eye on the deeper learning beyond the ritual of examination preparation. The joy of PRU teaching is that the culture of learning for the 'whole child', the focus on personal development, on building self-confidence and self-esteem, are alive and kicking. PRUs are places where adults who want to educate young people can practise their craft. Many mainstream schools have lost their joy; it has been squeezed out of them by a regime of mass inspection that is antithetical to the acquisition of quality. We have as a profession become so anxious about measures of attainment that we pass this anxiety down to the learners; we attempt to motivate children by repeatedly telling them that they are underachieving.

 Key points to remember

- Children in a PRU need very skilled adults to help them learn – good subject knowledge is a long way from being enough.
- For the right teachers they can be a place to learn and be creative.
- The stakes are high, our prisons are full of young men who were excluded from schools – if you have what it takes, teaching in a PRU is compelling and rewarding.
- PRUs need to recruit the very best – if you cannot teach mainstream top set year 11 in your own subject you have no business teaching! But if you can teach hard-man Josh to read or convince 13-year-old Texas that getting pregnant is not smart, we need you!

Additional resources

As well as the resources you'll find at **www.sagepub.co.uk/martindenham** you should also take a look at the following:

Bombèr, L. (2007) *Inside I'm Hurting: Practical Strategies for Supporting Children with Attachment Difficulties in School.* London: Worth. This book provides educational professionals with a classroom handbook of strategies, practical tools and for supporting children from an attachment perspective to promote inclusion in the school system.

Holt, J. (1982) *How Children Fail*, 2nd edn. St Ives: Penguin. This book is essential reading as it explores the reasons why children fail in school. Although this second edition was published in 1982 the content is still relevant, though some of the terminology would no longer be used today.

Pirsig, R. (1991) *Zen and the Art of Motorcycle Maintenance: An Inquiry into Values.* London: Vintage. This philosophical book is a journey with a father and his son.

CHAPTER 16

THE PARTICULAR NEEDS OF LOOKED AFTER CHILDREN

Caroline Walker-Gleaves

Key ideas explored in this chapter

- Who are looked after children?
- How does a child become looked after?
- Do looked after children have specific and unique educational and social difficulties or needs?
- Approaches to teaching and learning for children and young people who are looked after
- Considerations

Who are looked after children?

The term 'looked after children' is used to refer to that group of children whose parent is the state or the government, but the precise definition depends upon the exact legislation used, which differs between England, Northern Ireland, Scotland and Wales. Usually the definition covers all those children who are subject to what is called a 'care order', and are therefore 'taken into care'. There are other children temporarily classed as being looked after because of circumstances such as being on a short break or in 'respite care'. Children may also be looked after for other important reasons, for example, if they are 'unaccompanied minors' whose parents may have refugee or asylum seeker status. The term 'looked after' is also often used to describe what are known as 'accommodated children' who may be looked after on a voluntary basis at the request of, or with permission from, their parents.

The terms 'looked after' and 'in care' are often used interchangeably, but they mean slightly different things in practice. 'Looked after' is usually reserved for children who are subject to a care order and is a term that has legal significance, as set out in the Children Act of 1989. This Act recognised that looked after children have experiences and difficulties that other children simply do not, and that may reduce their life chances and act as barriers to achieving as much as other children. With this in mind, the provisions of the 1989 Act state that:

> Looked after children deserve the best experiences in life, from excellent parenting which promotes good health and educational attainment, to a wide range of opportunities to develop their talents and skills in order to have an enjoyable childhood and successful adult life (HM Government, 1989: 1).

The previous UK government (1997–2010), with its prioritisation of social justice and equality, passed very significant legislation aiming to improve the life and educational chances of children in public care (DfES, 2007; DCSF, 2009a, 2000b, 2009c). The former government also recognised, however, that the familial, cultural and wider social setting of many children was a contributory factor to eventual educational achievement: the Childcare Act of 2006 initiated provision for Sure Start centres, whose explicit aim was to provide early 'educare' for children in an attempt to address educational and social inequalities (HM Government, 2006). In addition, all schools have a statutory responsibility to promote the achievement of children who are looked after, including the provision of a designated teacher. The most recent UK government has continued the policy of social reform in education, the pupil premium being introduced in April 2011 as a way to target educational underachievement at individual school level, for children in poor socio-economic circumstances, children with parents in the armed forces, and children in public care. In summary, over the last decade a series of measures has been introduced that has explicitly attended to the vision of a more inclusive English schooling system for all children who are vulnerable by virtue of their personal, home and wider socio-economic and cultural circumstances.

 Key points to remember

- When children become 'looked after' they are subject to a 'care order'.
- There are many reasons that children are taken into care, such as possible harm, giving parental respite or being an unaccompanied minor.
- Children and young people from care may need greater support and encouragement than other young people in order to succeed in education and employment.

CASE STUDY

Sharing concerns

Kenzie first came to the attention of his class teacher at primary school when he would arrive in the morning with huge dark circles under his eyes and was yawning non-stop. Kenzie, who was aged 10 years at the time, was a very able young boy who was previously happy and smiling and full of energy. However, within a year, he had become withdrawn, tired and non-communicative. His class teacher mentioned this to the head teacher, who quite by chance had received a phone call from the LA social worker. It turned out that Kenzie's mother had bipolar disorder and that she had stopped taking medication after Kenzie's father, an accountant, had committed suicide due to an allegation of financial mismanagement. Kenzie's mother could not emotionally support Kenzie on her own, and in fact Kenzie had turned into his mother's carer, doing all the shopping, cleaning and cooking. Kenzie's mother's GP had informed Social Services and they had in turn informed the school. Kenzie was put into respite foster care close to his home, and his mother was given a package of mental health support including a community psychiatric nurse and cognitive behavioural therapy to help her to structure her own medication and mental health planning. The care plan for Kenzie was to be kept under review, with the aim for him to return home permanently in the near future.

How could you support this pupil?

- Understand that children encountering loss and change can mean that security and nurturing are more important in contexts where they may spend a lot of time, such as school.
- Provide ways in which such children can develop resilience, for example celebrating their achievements in class, making a point of showcasing all children's talents and interests, and promoting caring relationships in class, whether through positive friendships or nurturing environments.
- Give children an opportunity to develop and reflect on coherent stories about their lives through activities such as film making, digital storytelling, cartoon drawing. Any opportunity for children to think about what has happened and is happening to them should be taken.

How does a child become looked after?

Government statistics and research demonstrate that the majority of children coming into care – and as a result, the children who will ultimately be 'looked after' – will have a history of physical, sexual or psychological abuse, and alongside that will usually have experienced significant neglect. Abuse and neglect can take many forms, including physical, psychological and sexual abuse, and also neglect by virtue of hygiene, nutrition or withholding of needs such as attachment or nurture.

Figure 16.1 shows the origin of care-need for children becoming looked after in 2012.

It is clear from the diagram that not only are the reasons that most children will become looked after quite overlapping, but also that they will have profound consequences on children, mostly centred upon loss and grief. For example, children who have experienced abuse and neglect may also be experiencing family dysfunction, such as domestic violence or alcohol or drug abuse. Children whose families are in acute stress, such as through poverty or parental incarceration, may also be experiencing associated family illness such as depression (Brandon et al., 2008). What is very important to point out, though, is that contrary to many depictions of looked after children in the media and in literature and film as 'difficult' or 'damaged' children who cause problems in society, this is simply not the case. Only a very small number of children are in care because of crimes they have committed, and even then, examination of the history of such children almost always exposes family dysfunction (Lanius et al., 2010).

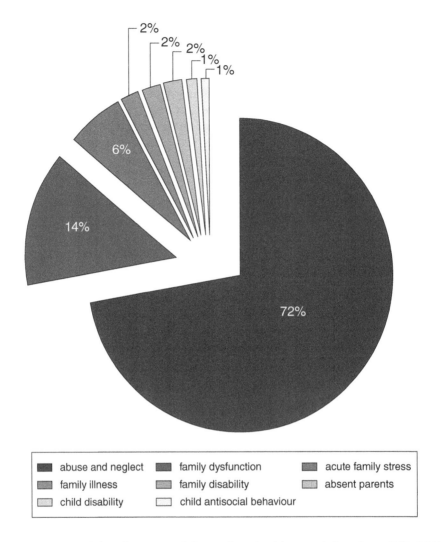

Figure 16.1 Origin of care-need (reproduced with permission from DfE, 2012c © Crown Copyright)

So, how do children come into care in the first place? Children come into care by two main routes: because the parents have asked for help or because the child is in danger of being harmed, usually either through abuse or neglect or a combination of these and other factors. When this happens, legislation is used to determine what will ultimately happen to a child:

> Where parents have asked for help, because for some reason their child can no longer stay at home, suitable accommodation is found for a child. Parental responsibility remains with the parent/guardian.

Usual reasons for help being sought include parental illness or disability, poverty, homelessness or parental incarceration (HM Government, 1989, s. 20).

If a child is in danger of being harmed, a court will make a 'Care Order'. The court will take all the circumstances into careful consideration before doing this. When a Care Order is made, children's services acquire parental responsibility and the state becomes a legal parent alongside the parent/guardian (HM Government, 1989, s. 31).

In both cases, an assessment is carried out by the LA to ascertain a child's particular circumstances and to make a longer-term care plan with the family and child (if the child is able to understand). This may include either returning a child to the family home, putting in place a range of support to assist the family if in crisis, or, if it is judged that the best outcome for a child is to remain out of the family structure, to make arrangements for permanent accommodation elsewhere, either a residential home, fostering or adoption. In this case an 'adoption order' is made and the child's parents change in law to the adoptive parents. When this happens, a child is also issued with a new birth certificate with their adopted family name.

  Key points to remember

- The vast majority of children are looked after due to abuse and neglect.
- When a child is placed in care, it is a complex process that is carried out with a range of professionals with responsibilities for a child's health, education, accommodation and safety.
- When a care order is made, the state becomes a legal parent alongside the parent/guardian.

CASE STUDY

Complex circumstances

Shahida is a 13-year-old girl who was taken into care when she was eight years old. She lived alone with her birth father, who was 84 and had Alzheimer's

(Continued)

(Continued)

disease. Her birth mother died when she was six, from liver disease caused by chronic alcoholism. Her teacher at primary school noticed that on many occasions Shahida arrived at school in dirty and smelly clothes so there were concerns about Shahida's cleanliness and hygiene. The school contacted Social Services who knew about Shahida but had found that her father had limited English and found it difficult to accept support for Shahida as well as accessing appropriate support for his own needs. Generally, he was unable to manage properly because of his condition. In addition, he was infirm and so unable to shop and provide food and support for Shahida. A Section 20 Care Order was eventually made and Shahida was found temporary accommodation in residential childcare until a foster placement was found.

How could you support this pupil?

- Remember that the social, cultural and home lives of children are very diverse, and when children come into your class with behaviours and appearances that you may consider to be unusual, you must always think very critically about what circumstances lie behind them.
- Discuss any concerns you have with other teachers, including specialist teachers and the head teacher, and find out whether concerns about the child are more widespread and serious.
- Focus on the educational and behavioural issues that are of concern to you as a teacher, whilst being aware of the background social and familial circumstances. If you become involved in a review of a child's progress or with meeting a key or social worker, it is important that you use plans and notes that you have been keeping to ensure a consistent and coherent approach.

Do looked after children have specific and unique educational and social difficulties or needs?

Children who are looked after are one of the most diverse yet uniquely vulnerable groups of children in any society. In the UK, many such children present a complex picture of underachievement and frequent disengagement in educational, social and health contexts. Their educational progress in particular is a cause for concern at all stages of schooling: studies consistently identify a number of factors correlated to significant levels of educational underachievement in many cases beginning in the early years, including school absence and transience, poor language development, and poor social functioning with peers. In terms of actual achievement, in 2013, 67.8 per cent of the 29,300 children who had been looked after for at least one year in England had an officially diagnosed statement of SEN, as compared with 18.8 per cent of all other pupils. At age 16, the gap between formal academic attainment is as wide: in 2013, 36.6 per cent of children in public care achieved five intermediate level qualifications (GCSEs) as compared with 80.3 per cent of all other children. Of those children in public care with statements of special educational need, only 2.8 per cent achieved this level of qualification (HM Government, 2014b). Such figures illustrate that the educational attainments of this group of children are lower than for any other group in British society.

The key issue for teachers, however, is to ask what is different about looked after children that make them so vulnerable and have such poor outcomes? First of all, children and young people entering care are very likely to have been abused or neglected, as we have seen previously.

The impact of abuse and neglect falls into three main areas:

- Health and physical effects, e.g. poor dental health, poor hearing.
- Intellectual and cognitive development, e.g. foetal alcohol syndrome, poor language and linguistic development.
- Emotional, psychological and behavioural consequences, e.g. low self-esteem, self-harming.

Apart from the most well-known impacts, however, there are other issues that can catastrophically affect looked after children's outcomes. One such is attachment, and the ways in which children experience and make stable relationships with caregivers when they are young. When attachment is disturbed, children may develop chaotic behaviours about who is looking after them and why, and not be able to understand developmental stages such as safe play, boundary formation and emotional regulation (Berridge, 2007). All of these are critical parts of a child's development as they enter school and begin to socialise, so it is perhaps unsurprising that many children who have been abused or neglected find education a troubling and uncertain place with expectations of behaviour that are unknown to them (Dearden, 2004).

There are looked after children who do thrive and succeed. Why? We know that the concept of resilience, or being able to cope with diversity and endure difficulty, is extremely important (Ward, 2011).

Research identifies several factors looked after children who have prevailed, experienced by including:

- positive experiences in school;
- healthy friendships;
- talents and interests;
- a committed adult who takes a strong and enduring interest in the child.

 Key points to remember

- Looked after children have very poor educational outcomes when compared with all other children, and a much higher proportion of classification of special needs.
- Looked after children may often 'internalise' their circumstances, either blaming themselves for things that have happened in that way, or thinking that they have no control over things that happen to them.
- Moving attention away from a focus purely on children's problems and towards a focus on developmental strengths, abilities and talents of looked after children and young people enables them to better cope with adversity.

CASE STUDY

The impact of adoption

Ade was a 15-year-old boy who was placed in care when he was seven years old. Prior to that he lived with his birth mother and her boyfriend. His birth mother was a drug user and prostitute and her boyfriend was a member of an organised violence gang at football matches who had previous convictions for grievous bodily harm and possession of firearms. When Ade was taken into care, under a Section 31 care order, he was functionally illiterate, he had hearing impairments caused by physical injury to his inner ear, and he was also prone to physically violent outbursts. Ade was placed in foster care initially, but his violence became difficult for foster carers to manage and he had a series of placements over the next four years. He also had poor educational outcomes, and remained unable to read or write proficiently at age 11, when he was offered for adoption by his LA. He was subsequently adopted and although he suffers from mental health difficulties (self-harming and multiple suicide attempts), intensive psychiatric support, a strong family and wider friendship circle, and a steady educational support system (comprising pastoral support in school and an online tutor in the evenings) have meant that Ade's progress in all areas is now good.

How could you support this pupil?

- Children with complex difficulties often present such formidable challenges that it is hard to know where to start. The best place is in forming a relationship with them. Make it clear, through talking and creating space for discussion, that you are open to talking about any difficulties at any time within the school day.
- Children such as Ade often have multiple social and mental health issues, for example a common one is obsessive compulsive disorder (OCD). For example, Ade finds it difficult to do things quickly, like dressing after PE or games, because he has to check things many times. Therefore do not organise your classroom always based on time-constrained activities, and give space for doing things slowly and carefully.
- When children begin to get anxious about particular incidents in class, ensure that your behaviour is calming and de-escalating, giving children space to calm down and regulate their emotions gradually.

Approaches to teaching and learning for children and young people who are looked after

There is limited research into the classroom consequences of teachers' beliefs but what there is suggests that there are problems in the way that teachers construct theories of behaviour and ability in relation to looked after children (Walker-Gleaves and Walker, 2008). Often teachers want to develop children's abilities and progression but report that they don't know how to. Teachers often lack the very specific psychological and practical knowledge needed to understand and deal with major issues such as grief, mental illness and self-harming. This can create an overwhelming 'basic survival' mindset in which educational progress remains relatively unimportant when compared with looked after children's safety and the need to 'protect' them from the pressure of testing and achievement.

Research shows that many teachers misunderstand these young people's emotional health and mistakenly attribute all their behaviours to traumatic incidents in their life histories, rather than seeing them as a function of stages in child development terms. Not only that, studies show that there is a misunderstanding about why children are looked after, and there is evidence that a much greater proportion who do have emotional and behavioural difficulties are disciplined much more frequently than other children, many eventually getting labels of 'conduct disordered', which in turn triggered automatic referral to a PRU. Linked to this, looked after children have a much greater number of exclusions from school than all other children.

Despite these difficulties, most trainee teachers are capable of extremely insightful worldviews concerning looked after children. The most effective teaching of looked after children (and all children) is 'inclusive' teaching; that is, based on the principle of 'head', 'hand' and 'heart', or the development of knowledge alongside appropriate practices, but ones that are based on critical beliefs about how to help children progress and thrive (Florian et al., 2010). Examples of such strategies are:

Knowing about (Head):

- teaching strategies;
- individual children's unique circumstances and needs;
- how children learn;
- the social and cultural contexts of children's lives.

Doing (Hand):

- translating individual knowledge into action;
- using evidence to improve your practice;
- learning how to work with other professionals;
- taking responsibility for your decisions and actions.

Believing (Heart):

- that all children are worth educating;
- that all children can learn;

- that all teachers can make a difference in children's lives;
- that teaching all children is the responsibility of all teachers.

 Key points to remember

- Do not make assumptions about looked after children's abilities and motivations to do well in school simply because of their 'looked after' status.
- Do not assume that professional responsibility for the progress and achievement of looked after children lies with other professionals, such as social workers, SENCOs and educational psychologists. It is frequently a function of professional knowledge and awareness of individual teachers within the school that ultimately leads to positive decisions and outcomes about looked after children's educational assessments.
- Understand that inclusive classroom practices are the most effective ways of teaching children with multiple and complex difficulties.

CASE STUDY

The impact of sexual abuse

Rikki's behaviour first came to the attention of her teachers in primary school. She was often disruptive in class and aggressive towards other children wanting to play. She had bruising on her legs that was visible during swimming and PE and frequently complained of pains in her abdomen. At home-times she would often remain in class and refuse to go into the school yard to be picked up. Rikki's teacher raised her concerns with the head teacher and they spoke to Rikki's older brother, who regularly picked her up from school. Involvement of Social Services led Rikki to be placed in emergency foster care and as a result of this, a police-instigated medical examination established long-term sexual abuse by the brother who was picking her up from school each night. Her brother was charged with sexual offences and Rikki was placed in long-term foster care. She continues to be very withdrawn in school, and is detached in class. She also refuses to eat at school and has begun to develop self-harming behaviour. She is now eight years old and has specialist support in school for literacy and numeracy. She also sees an educational psychologist once a week as well as having therapy for sexually abused children.

How could you support this pupil?

- You need to have strategies to find out how the child is feeling. Begin each class with a statement on how you and they feel, and include all children.
- Structure learning and teaching activities to maximise co-operation and kindness towards each other. Introduce conflict resolution as a way to solve problems and decide what to do when working and learning together. Introduce every possible means of peer mediation and discussing things together.
- Try to introduce activities early on in the day, since for a child who is not eating, any activity later on in the day may be exhausting and simply too demanding.

 Reflective activity

What are the main issues that affect the educational progress of looked after children? As a class teacher, what do you need to consider in terms of your practice, teaching strategies and pastoral care of a looked after child?

Considerations

The main issues that affect the educational progress of looked after children are related to understanding that the needs and experiences of this group of children are complex, but that trying to change your focus away from seeing everything as a 'problem' to seeing how you can help to develop strengths and abilities is an important key. There are two very important things that you, as a class teacher, can focus on, and both contribute towards supporting the development of emotional and social strengths that help looked after children blossom and prevail longer term. These things are *resilience* and *relationships*.

In terms of resilience, looked after children may well have experienced loss or disadvantage in their backgrounds, and struggled to have success or find people or experiences that make them happy and feel fulfilled. In developing children's interests in a variety of areas, or in finding things that they can be successful at and achieve, looked after children can develop self-esteem and self-worth in one area which then serves as a resilience-building activity for trying out other activities and for trying in other areas.

Similarly with relationships: teachers and other professionals can offer caring and enduring relationships, to make sure that school is a positive experience, and in classes to make sure that the experiences and contributions of all children are valued. This might be through talking activities, through taking the time to hear the experiences of all children, through ensuring that all children have the opportunity to contribute to 'show and tell' activities, to making your classroom inclusive through making sure that you greet and wait for all the children in your class equally.

Additional resources

As well as the resources you'll find at **www.sagepub.co.uk/martindenham** you should also take a look at the following:

Berridge, D. (2007) Theory and explanation in child welfare: education and looked after children, *Child and Family Social Work*, 12: 1–10. This is an important essay on why looked after children's learning success is as much a social as an educational issue for teachers.

Brandon, M., Belderson, P., Warren, C., Howe, D., Gardner, R., Dodsworth, J. and Black, J. (2008) *Analysing Child Deaths and Serious Injury Through Abuse and Neglect: What Can We Learn? A Biennial Analysis of Serious Case Review, 2003–2005*. London: DCSF. This is an analysis of the extent of abuse and injury in childhood, and an explanation of how much there is still to learn about serious abuse.

Florian, L., Young, K. and Rouse, M. (2010) Preparing teachers for inclusive and diverse educational environments: studying curricular reform in an Initial Teacher Education Course, *International Journal of Inclusive Education*, 14(7): 709–22. This is a research paper that discusses how teachers' inclusive teaching may improve the education of all children, but also how trainee teachers might think about what inclusion means for them individually.

Ward, H. (2011) Continuities and discontinuities: issues concerning the establishment of a persistent sense of self amongst care leavers, *Children and Youth Services Review*, 33: 2512–18. This study presents an argument about how being looked after might lead to damaging problems of self-esteem and self-respect throughout a person's life. It discusses how resilience might help to build a stronger sense of self into adulthood.

CHAPTER 17

REFLECTIONS OF TEACHING PUPILS WITH SPECIAL EDUCATIONAL NEEDS BY RECENTLY QUALIFIED TEACHERS

Rebecca Dunn, Helen Lowes and David Nevins

Rebecca, Helen and David qualified as primary school teachers in July 2013 following the successful completion of their BA (Hons) in Primary Education at the University of Sunderland. Having studied their teacher training degree for four years, they completed four successful teaching placements in mainstream primary schools and participated in a range of voluntary experiences in specialist provisions.

The intention of this chapter is for them to share their reflections of what it is like to be new to teaching pupils with special educational needs and/or disabilities (SEND).

Reflective account: Assembly

Rebecca Dunn, reflecting on a four-week teaching experience in a specialist context

School overview: The school was a large primary school that catered for pupils from 5 to 11 years with complex learning needs and pupils with autism.

One of the main differences in comparison to a mainstream school was the organisation of assembly. The pupils were supported by a high number of staff, sometimes one to one, to ensure that they could all participate and engage. In a mainstream context there is often the expectation that pupils will sit quietly and maintain concentration. In this particular context these expectations would have been unrealistic. Equipment and medication was available throughout assembly to support the pupils should the need arise. Another notable difference was that pupils would get up and walk around or move seats. For example, Inderjeet kept standing up running around the hall, then he would come back to his seat. He was closely observed by the staff team to ensure that he and others remained safe.

Singing was a regular feature in assembly to establish a calm and joyful environment. It was also used in the classrooms to calm the pupils and bring them to the area the teacher wanted them to be in. I was in a Key Stage 1 class of approximately seven pupils with autism and every lesson would start with a short song. Singing would also be used if a pupil became upset or distressed. It soon became clear to me that this was a very effective strategy to use and that the pupils responded well to a calm jubilant singing voice and would become compliant and engaged.

This experience provided me with a range of teaching and learning strategies which I have transferred to the mainstream context where I now work. I gained confidence in using a range of voice tones and singing as a behaviour management strategy which has proved to be highly effective.

 Key points to remember

- Take every opportunity you can to observe other practitioners and note the effective teaching and learning strategies they use.
- Use singing to manage pupils' behaviour in a positive way.

Reflective account: Multi-agency teams, teaching strategies and useful resources

David Nevins, reflecting on a four-week teaching experience in a specialist context

School overview: The school catered for pupils with autism and pervasive developmental disorder. The school was a day and residential

(Continued)

(Continued)

school for pupils aged from 3 to 19 years. The majority of the teaching practice occurred in a year 1 class of eight pupils.

During my pre-visit to the school it soon became apparent how complex the needs of each individual pupil in the school and class were. In preparation for the placement I learnt about the theory of the autistic spectrum; however, when completing my teaching experience it became apparent that whilst some characteristics were evident in some pupils, they all had very different individual needs.

The classroom teacher that I worked with had an excellent relationship with the support staff in the class and they worked extremely well together to provide an environment that was welcoming, friendly and conducive to learning. During the placement I also worked with and attended meetings and therapy sessions with other professionals such as the occupational therapist, the speech and language therapist and the educational psychologist. It was clear that the staff in the school and other professionals worked closely together, focussing on the education, welfare and support for each individual pupil. Due to the exposure of working with other professionals, this experience enabled me to consolidate some of the theoretical aspects of providing support to pupils with SEND that I studied at University.

Communication and routines

I observed and used PECS® to communicate with the pupils. The school also used signing to develop the communication skills of each pupil. During snack time the behaviour of the pupils in the class improved, it became evident that food was a motivator. For example, Daniel would regularly attempt to try to climb around the classroom during free time and would rarely respond to communication attempts from an adult. However, during the snack time session Daniel sat calmly, became attentive and used PECS®. He enjoyed the reward of taking ownership of ordering his own food using the PECS®. This became an ideal time to develop Daniel's non-verbal communication skills using this communication system.

Reading and PECS®

During the placement I chose to observe how the pupils in the class use literature to aid learning. During an activity I observed a one-to-one 'colour semantics' session between a pupil called Aurek and a member of the support team which involved the use of an Oxford Reading

Tree book. The learning objective of the lesson was to understand 'Who is it?' using the characters contained in the story. Two A4 PECS® holders were used; one contained the PECS® cards of the characters in the story (coloured in orange) and the other contained the action that the character was doing (i.e. brushing hair, opening the door – coloured in yellow). The sentence strip contained an orange and a yellow holder card. The support staff read a page at a time and asked Aurek 'Who is it?', Aurek had to choose the character using the PECS® card and place this on the associated colour on the sentence strip holder. The same was repeated for the action. The use of 'Working towards' cards was helpful in teaching Aurek, as this helped him to focus on the activity. As a reward for an appropriate response he received a sticker to place on his 'Working towards' chart when correct responses were given. I found the observation useful as due to the ability levels of the pupils in the class I had no prior understanding of how it would be possible to engage the pupils in reading. The observation led me to facilitate colour semantics sessions myself during the course of the placement, where I also prepared appropriate resources for different stories that engaged each individual pupil based on their interests. This also led me to use sensory storytelling techniques, where the pupils handled objects, smelt different scents and listened to different sounds that were all associated to the story being read, all of which helped to enable them to understand the story. Story sequencing using PECS® cards that illustrated the different stages of the story also enabled pupils like Aurek to retell the story using this communication method.

Reflective account: Managing barriers to learning

Helen Lowes, reflecting on a four-week teaching experience in a specialist context

School overview: The school catered for pupils with autistic spectrum disorders, learning difficulties, behavioural, emotional and social difficulties and profound and multiple learning difficulties. The school provides education for pupils ranging from Nursery to Sixth form.

On arrival I was introduced to the host class teacher which was followed by meeting the pupils in the nursery setting. Although I was prepared from the pre-visit, it was clearly apparent that the range of needs in the classroom both medically and educationally was

(Continued)

(Continued)

immense. Throughout my experience at the school I worked specifically with two pupils with attachment difficulties.

In order to ensure that the pupils were supported appropriately in school, I spent time observing routines, behaviour, teaching and learning. This was achieved by organising and providing a nurturing, fun and educational environment with appropriate boundaries of behaviour. This is where my organisational and time management skills were challenged. I had to adapt activities I thought were creative and interesting that I would use in mainstream provision to match the pupil's capabilities and profile, for example having a tray of items to help identify initial phonemes in words and recognising other words to match that phoneme to enable the pupil to write a sentence. This was to maximise the educational and social outcomes through identification and reduction of barriers to learning.

Promoting positive behaviour

At times the pupils were challenging and could be unpredictable; for example, Tom found it hard to share my time with Emma or other pupils, this resulted in him hitting her or others and using abusive language. The usual methods of de-escalating his behaviour were ineffective. The situation then escalated, causing Tom to hit and kick Emma, the outcome being that he needed to be restrained for his safety and that of the others by the class teacher and a member of the support staff. Within 30 minutes Tom was able to re-join the class, which then allowed me to demonstrate what was expected from him. I was able to analyse the situation and suggest the next steps, which was to take Tom to his preferred place whilst calmly talking to him and returning to a different task on his return.

Developing self-esteem

I spent time developing Emma's self-esteem and sense of belonging through interaction with other pupils, the use of games, building positive relationships with adults and coping strategies like 'zone time' where she would go to calm down. It was challenging when Emma found it difficult to cope and became distressed, which sometimes caused her to have an epileptic seizure and required medication to be administered. This experience allowed me to recognise how a situation can escalate and how teachers should be aware of not only educational needs for each pupil but also their medical needs.

The time I spent in the specialist provision allowed me to build my own confidence and understanding of how to deal with complex situations and how to build the pupils' self-esteem by providing appropriate and stimulating activities for each pupil. It also allowed me to think creatively about what activities would meet the pupils' needs.

 Key points to remember

- Provide the school with a photograph of yourself before you start, as some pupils will be sensitive to change and this will allow the home class teacher to introduce you before your visit.
- Be prepared to see a large amount of specialist equipment used, including medical equipment; for example, some pupils may be on oxygen or fed through a tube.
- Be open-minded and expect the unexpected.
- Ensure that you arrange a pre-visit to the school and the class you will be working with.
- During pre-visit observe routines and behaviour of the pupils. Take note of how the pupils emotionally regulate and how the staff facilitate this.
- Read the school's Ofsted report and visit the school website.
- Be prepared to observe Team-Teach strategies to protect the pupils from harming themselves and others.
- Have the expectation of staff-to-pupil ratios being significantly higher than in a mainstream setting.
- Avoid becoming overly attached to the pupils.
- Use the pupils' targets and other school initiatives/programmes to inform planning.

Additional resources

As well as the resources you'll find at **www.sagepub.co.uk/martindenham** you should also take a look at the following:

SEN Teacher Free Learning Materials (2013), available at http://www. senteacher.org/: This website includes a range of resources, such as software and teaching resources, which are free to download for pupils 5–16 years.

TESconnect, available at www.tes.co.uk/sen-teaching-resources/: This website includes free learning resources for SEN teachers, including lesson plans, activities, games, teaching ideas, classroom resources and worksheets.

REFERENCES

Abrahams, B.S and Geschwind, D.H. (2008) Advances in autism genetics: on the threshold of a new neurobiology, *Nature Reviews: Genetics*, 9(5): 341–55.

Berridge, D. (2007) Theory and explanation in child welfare: education and looked after children, *Child and Family Social Work*, 12: 1–10.

Brandon, M., Belderson, P., Warren, C., Howe, D., Gardner, R., Dodsworth, J. and Black, J. (2008) *Analysing Child Deaths and Serious Injury Through Abuse and Neglect: What Can We Learn? A Biennial Analysis of Serious Case Review, 2003–2005*. London: DCSF.

Bombèr, L. (2007) *Inside I'm Hurting: Practical Strategies for Supporting Children with Attachment Difficulties in School*. London: Worth.

Combley, M. (2000) *The Hickey Multi-sensory Language Course*, 3rd edn. London: Wiley-Blackwell.

Contact a Family (2014) Available at: www.cafamily.org.uk (accessed February 2015).

Dearden, J. (2004) Resilience: a study of risk and protective factors from the perspective of young people with experience of local authority care, *Support for Learning*, 19(4): 187–93.

Department of Children, Schools and Families (2008) *The Assessment for Learning Strategy.* Nottingham: DCSF.

Department for Children, Schools and Families (DCSF) (2009a) *Improving the Educational Attainment of Children in Care (Looked After Children)*. Nottingham: DCSF.

Department for Children, Schools and Families (DCSF) (2009b) *Improving the Attainment of Looked After Children in Primary Schools*. Nottingham: DCSF.

Department for Children, Schools and Families (DCSF) (2009c) *Improving the Attainment of Looked After Children in Secondary Schools*. Nottingham: DCSF.

Department for Education (DfE) (2010) *Progression 2010–2011: Advice on Improving Data to Raise Attainment and Maximise the Progress of Learners with Special Educational Needs*. London: DfE.

Department for Education (DfE) (2011a) *Teachers' Standards*. London: DfE.

Department for Education (DfE) (2011b) *P Scales: Level Descriptors P1 to P8*. London: DfE.

Department for Education (DfE) (2012a) *GCSE and Equivalent Attainment by Pupil Characteristics in England: 2010 to 2011*. London: DfE.

Department for Education (DfE) (2012b) *A Profile of Pupil Exclusions in England*. London: DfE.

Department for Education (DfE) (2012c) *Children Looked After by Local Authorities in England: Year Ending 31 March 2012*. Nottingham: DfE.

Department for Education (DfE) (2013a) *National Curriculum in England: Primary Curriculum*. London: DfE. Available at www.gov.uk/government/publications/national-curriculum-in-england-primary-curriculum (accessed August 2014).

Department for Education (DfE) (2013b) *National Curriculum in England: Secondary Curriculum*. London: DfE. Available at www.gov.uk/government/publications/national-curriculum-in-england-secondary-curriculum (accessed August 2014).

Department for Education (DfE) (2014a) *Special Educational Needs and Disability Code of Practice: 0–25 Years*. London: DfE.

Department for Education (DfE) (2014b) *Statutory Framework for the Early Years Foundation Stage (from 1 September 2014)*. London: DfE.

Department for Education (DfE) (2014c) *Performance-P Scale-Attainment Targets for Pupils with Special Educational Needs*. London: DfE.

Department for Education and Employment (2001) *Supporting the Target Setting Process: Guidance for Effective Target Setting for Pupils with Special Educational Needs*. Nottingham: DfEE Publications.

Department for Education and Skills (DfES) (2007) *Care Matters: Transforming the Lives of Children and Young People in Care (Green Paper)*. London: The Stationery Office.

Department of Children, Schools and Families (DCSF) (2008) *The Assessment for Learning Strategy*. Nottingham: DCSF.

Diabetes UK (2014) Available at: www.diabetes.org.uk (accessed February 2015).

Early Education (2012) *Development Matters in the Early Years Foundation Stage*. London: British Association for Early Childhood Education. Available at www.early-education.org.uk/development-matters (accessed July 2014).

Emerson, J. (2013) *The Dyscalculia Assessment*. London: Bloomsbury Educational.

Florian, L., Young, K. and Rouse, M. (2010) Preparing teachers for inclusive and diverse educational environments: studying curricular reform in an Initial Teacher Education Course, *International Journal of Inclusive Education*, 14(7): 709–72.

Geddes, H. (2006) *Attachment in the Classroom: The Link Between Children's Early Experience, Emotional Wellbeing and Performance in School*. London: Worth.

Genetic Disorders UK (2014) Available at: www.geneticdisordersuk. org (accessed February 2015).

Hannell, G. (2005) *Dyscalculia: Action Plans for Successful Learning in Mathematics*. London: David Fulton.

Hatcher, P.J., Duff, F.J. and Hulme, C. (2014) *Sound Linkage: An Integrated Programme for Overcoming Reading Difficulties*. London: Wiley-Blackwell.

HM Government (1989) *Children Act 1989 as originally enacted*. Available at www.legislation.gov.uk (accessed December 2013).

HM Government (2006) *Childcare Act 2006 as originally enacted*. Available at www.legislation.gov.uk (accessed December 2013).

HM Government (2014a) *Children and Families Act 2014*. London: The Stationery Office.

HM Government (2014b) *Outcomes for Children Looked After by Local Authorities*. London: The Stationery Office. Available at www.gov. uk/government/collections/statistics-looked-after-children (accessed January 2014).

Holt, J. (1982) *How Children Fail*, 2nd edn. St Ives: Penguin.

International Dyslexia Association (2008) Available at: http://eida. org/ (accessed February 2015).

Kanner, L. (1943) Autistic disturbance of affective contact, *Nervous Child*, 2: 217–50. Available at http://neurodiversity.com/library_ kanner_1943.html (accessed April 2014).

Kelly, K.S. and Phillips, S. (2011) *Teaching Literacy to Learners with Dyslexia: A Multi-sensory Approach*. London: SAGE.

Lanius, R.A., Vermetten, E. and Pain, C. (2010) *The Impact of Early Life Trauma on Health and Disease: The Hidden Epidemic*. Cambridge: Cambridge University Press.

Office for Standards in Education (Ofsted) (2013) *Unseen Children: Access and Achievement 20 Years On: Evidence Report*. London: Ofsted.

Office for Standards in Education (Ofsted) (2014) *The Framework for School Inspection*. London: Ofsted.

Phillips, S., Kelly, K.S. and Symes, L. (2013) *Assessment of Learners with Dyslexic Type Difficulties*. London: SAGE.

Pirsig, R. (1991) *Zen and the Art of Motorcycle Maintenance: An Inquiry into Values*. London: Vintage.

Rogers, B. (2011) *You Know The Fair Rule: Strategies for Positive and Effective Behaviour Management and Discipline in Schools*. London: Pearson.

Rogers, B. and McPherson, E. (2014) *Behaviour Management with Young Children: Crucial First Steps with Children 3–7 Years*, 2nd edn. London: SAGE.

Rogers, J. and Bourne, L. (2001) *Achieving Dyslexia Friendly Schools: Resource Pack*. London: British Dyslexia Association.

The Dyspraxia Foundation (2014) Available at: http://www.dyspraxia foundation.org.uk/about-dyspraxia (accessed February 2015).

The National Autistic Society (2014) Available at: www.autism.org.uk (accessed October 2014).

The National Health Service (NHS) (2014) Available at: www.nhs.uk (accessed February 2015).

Training and Development Agency (TDA) (2008) *Special Educational Needs and Disability: A Training Resource for Initial Teacher Training Primary Undergraduate Training Toolkit*. London: TDA.

UK Government (2014) *Outcomes for Children Looked After by Local Authorities*. Available at https://www.gov.uk/government/collections/statistics-looked-after.children (accessed January 2014).

Walker-Gleaves, A. and Walker, C. (2008) Imagining a different life in school: educating student teachers about 'looked after' children and young people, *Teachers and Teaching: Theory and Practice*, 14(5–6): 465–79.

Ward, H. (2011) Continuities and discontinuities: issues concerning the establishment of a persistent sense of self amongst care leavers, *Children and Youth Services Review*, 33: 2512–18.

Wing, L. and Gould, J. (1979) Severe impairments of social interaction and associated abnormalities in children: epidemiology and classification, *Journal of Autism and Developmental Disorders*, 9: 11–29.

INDEX